THE ROCK MONSTERS GUIDE TO DRUMS

CREATED BY DAVE LAZARUS
WITH
ANDY V. GALEON

ILLUSTRATION CREDITS:

ROCK STARS ... MARC TILL SCHMID
MONSTERS ... RICHARD CHAPLIN, JOVA GROF,
PRZEMYSLAW DEDELIS, OMAIK NIEV, GEORGE ZAPATA

WWW.THEROCKMONSTERS.COM

HOW TO USE THIS GUIDE

THE FIRST PART OF THIS GUIDE COVERS THE RUDIMENTS YOU WILL NEED TO KNOW TO BEGIN DEVELOPING YOUR HAND AND FOOT COORDINATION. START BY LEARNING TO PLAY THE HAND EXERCISES FIRST, AND THEN INTEGRATE THE FOOT PATTERNS TOGETHER. ONCE YOU HAVE THAT DOWN, YOU CAN ATTEMPT TO PLAY POLYRHYTHMS WITH EACH LIMB PLAYING INDEPENDENT PATTERNS TOGETHER ALL AT ONCE. DON'T WORRY, IT'S HARD AT FIRST BUT IT BECOMES SO MUCH FUN ONCE YOU CAN DO IT!

MEMORIZE THE RUDIMENTS AND PLAY THEM ON JUST THE SNARE DRUM, THEN ADD A TOM, THEN ADD A FLOOR TOM, THEN ADD A CYMBAL, THEN ADD A SECOND BASS DRUM, AND SO ON.

THE SECOND PART COVERS THE DRUM BEAT STYLES THAT YOU WILL NEED TO KNOW TO BE ABLE TO PLAY DIFFERENT STYLES OF MUSIC. MEMORIZE THE BEATS AND THEIR DISTINCT FEELS, AND LEARN HOW TO PLAY THEM ON THE DIFFERENT PARTS OF THE DRUM KIT. THEN GO STRAIGHT TO THE FILLS! PLAY THEM OVER AND OVER, STARTING OFF SLOW, THEN GOING AS FAST AS YOU CAN. THIS WILL GET YOU STARTED JAMMING ON THE DRUMS!

LOOK AT THE BOOK WHILE YOU JAM ... OPEN THE BOOK TO THE BEAT YOU WANT TO PLAY ... PUT ON THE SONG YOU WANT TO PLAY TO ... AND JAM WHILE LOOKING AT THE BEAT YOU ARE PLAYING. SEE THE ROCK, THE BLUES, THE SHUFFLE, THE METAL, THE FUNK, AND ALL THE DRUM FILLS. IN TIME YOU WILL GET TO KNOW THESE BEATS BY "FEEL" AND WON'T NEED TO USE THE BOOK.

GO TO THE ROCK MONSTERS WEBSITE AND WATCH THE VIDEOS !!!

EVERYTHING IS EASY TO UNDERSTAND WHEN YOU MATCH THE VIDEOS ON THE WEBSITE TO THE DIAGRAMS IN THIS BOOK. IT'S ALL THERE TO HELP *YOU*.

PRACTICE – RULE OF THUMB SAYS THAT IT TAKES 10,000 HOURS OF PRACTICE TO MASTER A SKILL. THAT MEANS PLAYING DRUMS 4 HOURS A DAY FOR 7 YEARS. (ALL THE GREAT DRUMMERS IN THIS GUIDE PLAYED THAT MUCH, IF NOT MORE.) YOU MIGHT NOT BE ABLE TO PRACTICE THAT MUCH, BUT YOU STILL NEED TO PUT IN THE TIME IT TAKES IF YOU WANT TO BE A GOOD DRUMMER. THERE'S NO SHORT CUTS. **PRACTICE EVERY DAY!!!**

IT'S BETTER TO PLAY 30 MINUTES EVERY DAY THAN 3 HOURS ONE DAY.

PLAYING EVERYDAY MAKES YOU DEVELOP THE TOUGH, HARD CALLUSES YOU NEED ON YOUR THUMB, INDEX FINGER, AND PALMS. THEN THE STICKS WON'T HURT, YOU'LL BE ABLE TO PLAY WITH PROPER TECHNIQUE, KEEP A TIGHTLY LOOSE GRIP, AND JAM!

ASK YOUR PARENTS TO READ THE **"GUIDE FOR PARENTS"** ON THE LAST PAGE.

IT'S CALLED "PLAYING" DRUMS BECAUSE IT'S ALL ABOUT HAVING FUN!

THE ROCK MONSTERS GUIDE TO DRUMS

LET'S GET ROCKIN'!

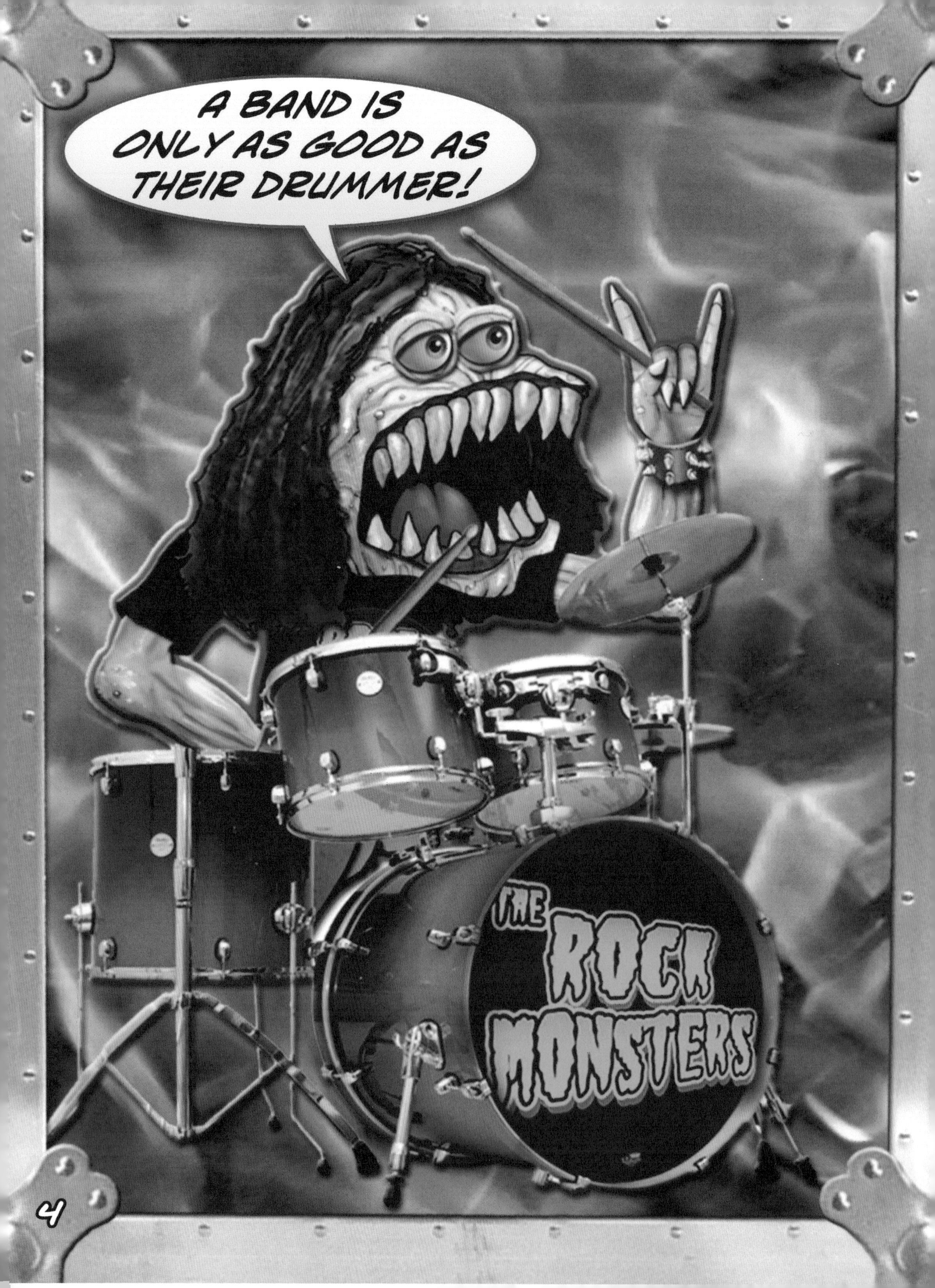
A BAND IS ONLY AS GOOD AS THEIR DRUMMER!
THE ROCK MONSTERS

THE DRUMMER

BEING A DRUMMER IS BEING PART OF A TRADITION THAT GOES BACK TO THE BEGINNING OF HUMAN HISTORY. PLAYING A RHYTHM WITH A STICK ON A HOLLOW LOG HAS BEEN HAPPENING FOR THE PAST 10,000 YEARS.

A REAL DRUMMER IS A SPECIAL PERSON. A REAL DRUMMER IS SOMEONE WHO FEELS THE RHYTHM AND WANTS TO POUND IT OUT. A REAL DRUMMER HAS A DIFFERENT MENTALITY ABOUT MUSIC. (AND TYPICALLY LIFE TOO!)

ALONG WITH THE BASS PLAYER YOU ARE "THE RHYTHM SECTION." YOUR GROOVE IS WHAT MAKES PEOPLE WANT TO MOVE, SHAKE, AND DANCE ... OR HEADBANG IN THE CASE OF HARD ROCK AND METAL!

LOCK IN WITH THE BASS PLAYER. LISTEN TO WHAT THE BASS PLAYER IS DOING AND TRY TO MATCH THAT WITH YOUR BASS DRUM.

PLAY FOR THE SONG. PLAY WHAT IS APPROPRIATE FOR THE SONG. DON'T SHOW OFF. (AT LEAST NOT ALL THE TIME!) A WELL PLACED FILL CAN ADD A LOT TO A SONG, AND A MISPLACED FILL (OR TOO MANY FILLS) CAN TAKE AWAY FROM THE FEELING OF THE SONG. WHEN IN DOUBT, LEAVE IT OUT.

AS THE DRUMMER YOU MUST BE THE CONSTANT TEMPO THE BAND DEPENDS ON TO BE STEADY AS A ROCK. DO NOT SPEED UP OR SLOW DOWN. PRACTICE WITH A METRONOME TO GET GOOD AT KEEPING TIME.

DON'T BE **"THE RUSSIAN DRAGON"** – EITHER RUSHING OR DRAGGING.

AS THE DRUMMER YOU MUST NEVER STOP PLAYING. WHEN YOU STOP, YOU STOP THE SONG. IF YOU LOSE IT, KEEP GOING UNTIL YOU CAN GET BACK ON THE BEAT.

AND BE COOL TO YOUR BANDMATES. THOSE DRUMS ARE SUPER LOUD! NOBODY CAN TALK IF YOU ARE PLAYING DRUMS. GETTING WARMED UP WITH A FEW FILLS IS COOL, BUT IF THAT IS THE ONLY TIME YOU ARE PRACTICING, THEN YOU ARE DEFINITELY NOT PRACTICING ENOUGH.

JOHN BONHAM

JOHN HENRY BONHAM WAS BORN ON MAY 31, 1948 IN REDDITCH, ENGLAND.

BONZO

IN 1953 JOHN BEGAN LEARNING TO PLAY DRUMS WHEN HE WAS FIVE, MAKING A DRUM KIT OUT OF CONTAINERS AND COFFEE TINS.

IN 1958, WHEN HE WAS TEN YEARS OLD, HIS MOTHER GAVE HIM A SNARE DRUM.

IN 1963 HIS FATHER BOUGHT HIM HIS FIRST DRUM KIT, A PREMIER. HE WAS 15.

JOHN NEVER TOOK ANY FORMAL DRUM LESSONS. AS A TEEN HE WOULD GET ADVICE FROM OTHER DRUMMERS.

JOHN'S BIGGEST INFLUENCES ARE GENE KRUPA AND BUDDY RICH.

IN 1964, JOHN JOINED HIS FIRST SEMI-PROFESSIONAL BAND WHO RELEASED A MODERATELY SUCCESSFUL SINGLE IN 1964. JOHN THEN TOOK UP DRUMMING FULL-TIME.

1966, HE JOINED A BLUES GROUP CALLED "CRAWLING KING SNAKES," WHOSE SINGER WAS ROBERT PLANT.

WHEN ROBERT DECIDED TO FORM "BAND OF JOY" IN 1967 JOHN WAS HIS FIRST CHOICE AS DRUMMER. BAND OF JOY RECORDED A NUMBER OF DEMOS BUT NO ALBUM.

IN 1968 AMERICAN SINGER TIM ROSE TOURED BRITAIN AND INVITED BAND OF JOY TO OPEN HIS CONCERTS. WHEN ROSE RETURNED TO ENGLAND FOR ANOTHER TOUR HE INVITED JOHN TO PLAY DRUMS IN HIS BAND.

AFTER THE BREAK-UP OF THE YARDBIRDS, GUITARIST JIMMY PAGE WAS FORMING A NEW BAND. WHEN ROBERT PLANT JOINED AS SINGER, ROBERT SUGGESTED JOHN ON DRUMS.

JOHN JOINED "THE NEW YARDBIRDS" IN 1968 BECAUSE HE LIKED THE MUSIC THEY PLAYED.

JOHN WAS 21 IN 1969 WHEN HE RECORDED THE FIRST LED ZEPPELIN ALBUM.

THE POCKET

THERE ARE THREE WAYS TO APPROACH **"THE BEAT"** ...
YOU CAN PLAY DEAD ON THE BEAT (SOUNDS "STIFF"), SLIGHTLY
AHEAD OF THE BEAT ("PUSHING"), OR SLIGHTLY BEHIND THE BEAT
("PULLING"). **"THE POCKET"** IS THE NANOSECOND IN TIME THAT
THE BEAT LASTS – FROM PULLING TO PUSHING.

WHEN A DRUMMER (OR BASS PLAYER, OR GUITAR PLAYER) IS
PLAYING VERY LAID BACK AND CREATING A "GROOVE," THEY ARE
PLAYING **"BEHIND THE BEAT."** RELAX AND LET THE MUSIC FLOW.

PLAYING **"BEHIND THE BEAT"** GIVES THE ILLUSION OF A SLOWER
TEMPO. IT'S ALMOST LIKE THE DRUMMER IS SLOWING DOWN THE
ENTIRE SONG, BUT HE'S NOT. LISTEN TO THE GUYS WHO PLAYED
WITH JAMES BROWN, THEY WOULD **LAY BACK** A LOT, WHICH GIVES
THE MUSIC A **FUNKY, GROOVY FEEL.** THAT IS PLAYING **"IN THE
POCKET."** LISTEN TO THE WAY JOHN BONHAM PLAYS DRUMS ON
"WHEN THE LEVEE BREAKS" OR "KASHMIR"... IT FEELS LIKE YOU
ARE WALKING THROUGH MUD. THAT IS PLAYING "BEHIND THE BEAT."

PLAYING **"AHEAD OF THE BEAT"** IS THE EXACT OPPOSITE. IT
CREATES A DRIVING, AGGRESSIVE FEELING, WHICH PUSHES THE
ENERGY FORWARD. IT'S ALMOST LIKE THE DRUMMER IS RUSHING,
BUT REALLY ISN'T RUSHING AT ALL. THIS IS THE WAY THAT MANY
MODERN METAL AND ROCK DRUMMERS PLAY TODAY.

AND THEN THERE IS **"SWING,"** WHERE THE DRUMMER WILL PUSH
AND PULL THE BEAT AT THE SAME TIME. THE BASS DRUM WILL BE
PUSHING AHEAD WHILE THE SNARE WILL LAG BEHIND. THE
CYMBALS REMAIN THE RHYTHMIC CENTER (DEAD ON THE BEAT.)

THE ONLY WAY TO LEARN HOW TO PLAY IN THE POCKET IS
THROUGH THE EXPERIENCE OF PLAYING WITH OTHER MUSICIANS.

THE HISTORY OF DRUMS 101

PRE-HISTORIC MAN PLAYED DRUMS...
EVERY CULTURE, ALL AROUND THE WORLD FROM THE DAWN OF TIME PLAYED DRUMS. DRUMS WERE AN IMPORTANT PART OF RITUALS AND RELIGIOUS CEREMONIES IN ANCIENT TRIBAL CULTURES. DIFFERENT TRIBES USED THE DRUMS TO EXPRESS THEMSELVES. PEOPLE USED DRUMS TO SEND MESSAGES TO EACH OTHER OVER VAST DISTANCES.

AS HUMANS TRANSITIONED FROM THE RHYTHMS OF HUNTING AND GATHERING TO THOSE OF SEEDING AND HARVESTING, THE DRUM MADE BORING, REPETITIVE WORK ALMOST FUN. WORK SONGS ARE USED TO PASS THE TIME AND ENERGIZE THE GROUP. THE PRODUCTIVITY OF A GROUP CAN OFTEN DEPEND ON THE TALENT OF THE MUSICIAN WHO ACCOMPANIES THEM. A GOOD MUSICIAN WILL HELP EVERYONE PASS THE TIME WITH THE MOVEMENT, RHYTHM AND NOISE MAKING HIM VALUABLE.

3,000 B.C. - 1800'S - DRUMS WERE USED TO SET THE PACE FOR MARCHING ARMIES AND ROWING OARSMEN. DRUMS WERE USED TO SIGNAL TROOPS DURING BATTLES.

DRUMS WERE THE DRIVING FORCE BEHIND ARMIES FOR CENTURIES. THE GOAL WAS TO ENERGIZE YOUR TROOPS WHILE TERRIFYING YOUR ENEMIES WITH THE THUNDEROUS NOISE YOU COULD MAKE. AS WARFARE GREW MORE COMPLEX, THE FUNCTION OF THE DRUM CHANGED. ARMIES DEVELOPED A SET OF DRUMMING PATTERNS THAT ALLOWED LEADERS TO COMMUNICATE VARIOUS MESSAGES TO THE TROOPS AND SIGNAL MANEUVERS.

1869 - THE RUDIMENTS CODIFIED
GARDINER A. STRUBE, A DRUM MAJOR IN THE ARMY, WROTE A BOOK WITH THE MOST POPULAR AND USEFUL PATTERNS HE LEARNED AND USED DURING HIS TIME IN THE ARMY. THIS BOOK, "THE STRUBES DRUM AND FIFE INSTRUCTOR," WAS ADOPTED BY THE U.S. ARMY AS THE MANUAL FOR TRAINING MILITARY FIELD MUSICIANS.

1900 – THE FIRST DRUM KITS WERE DEVELOPED IN NEW ORLEANS. DRUMMERS TOOK DIFFERENT MARCHING DRUMS AND SET THEM UP SO THEY COULD PLAY THEM TOGETHER.

1930'S – GENE KRUPA USED SLINGERLAND BRAND DRUMS. AT KRUPA'S URGING, SLINGERLAND DEVELOPED TOM-TOMS WITH TUNEABLE TOP AND BOTTOM HEADS, WHICH IMMEDIATELY BECAME IMPORTANT ELEMENTS OF VIRTUALLY EVERY DRUMMER'S SET-UP. KRUPA DEVELOPED AND POPULARIZED MANY OF THE CYMBAL TECHNIQUES THAT BECAME STANDARDS. HIS COLLABORATION WITH ARMAND ZILDJIAN OF THE AVEDIS ZILDJIAN COMPANY DEVELOPED THE MODERN HI-HAT CYMBALS AND STANDARDIZED THE NAMES AND USES OF THE RIDE, CRASH, SPLASH, PANG, AND SWISH CYMBALS.

1940'S – JAZZ DRUMS – GENE KRUPA, BUDDY RICH

1950'S – ROCK N' ROLL DRUMS
THE DEVELOPMENT OF "THE BACKBEAT."

1960'S – THE MODERN DRUM SET PERFECTED
ROCK DRUMMERS BEGAN TO DEVELOP THE DRUM KIT THAT IS CONSIDERED THE STANDARD TODAY... THEY ADDED MORE TOMS AND CYMBALS, AS WELL AS ANOTHER BASS DRUM TO BOOST SPEED. BY 1967 BOTH KEITH MOON AND GINGER BAKER PLAYED DRUM KITS WITH TWO BASS DRUMS.

1980'S – ELECTRONIC DRUMS ARE ALL THE RAGE.
ELECTRONIC DRUMS THEN CAME INTO BEING WITH THE INTENTION OF CREATING SOUNDS THAT ACOUSTIC DRUMS WERE UNABLE TO GENERATE.

1990'S – THE DOUBLE-BASS PEDAL BECOMES POPULAR.
2000'S – MODERN DRUMMING TECHNIQUE – FAST!

THE DRUMS

A TYPICAL 5-PIECE DRUM SET:

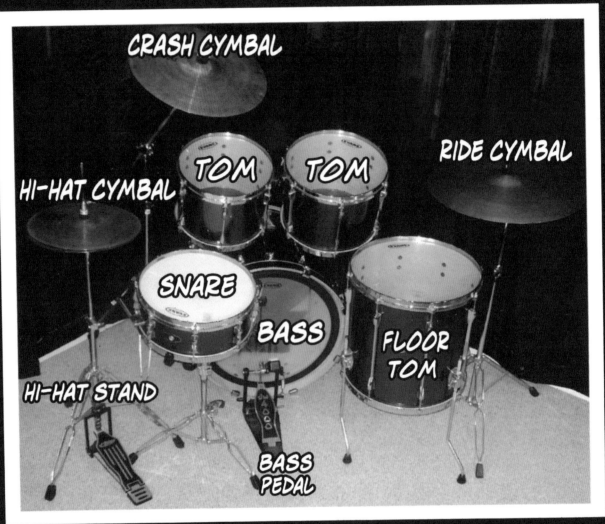

CRASH CYMBAL

RIDE CYMBAL

HI-HAT CYMBAL

TOM TOM

SNARE

BASS

FLOOR TOM

HI-HAT STAND

BASS PEDAL

ALTHOUGH DRUMS ARE ANCIENT, THE MODERN DRUM SET IS A RELATIVELY NEW INSTRUMNENT. OVER THE PAST 30 YEARS THERE HAVE BEEN RADICAL ADVANCEMENTS IN DRUM TECHNOLOGY AND TECHNIQUE TO ARRIVE AT THE PLACE WHERE IT IS TODAY.

YOU CAN ADD A DOUBLE-BASS PEDAL, MORE CYMBALS, A COWBELL, ANOTHER FLOOR TOM, CHIMES ... TO ENHANCE YOUR POSSIBILITIES, BUT THE 5 –PIECE IS ENOUGH TO GET YOU STARTED AND WILL REMAIN THE BASIS OF YOUR DRUM SET ALWAYS.

THE BASS DRUM

A.K.A. THE "KICK" DRUM. IT IS THE FOUNDATION FOR ALL YOUR DRUM BEATS. THE BASS DRUM ALWAYS LANDS ON THE "ONE" IN THE COUNT AND PROPELS THE RHYTHM OF THE WHOLE BAND. THE BASS DRUM IS THE BIG, LOW SOUND THAT MAKES PEOPLE WANT TO MOVE, SHAKE, AND DANCE.

THE BASS DRUM SITS ON THE FLOOR WITH THE "BATTER SIDE" (THE SIDE YOU HIT) TOWARD THE DRUMMER AND THE "RESONANT SIDE" (THE SIDE YOU DON'T HIT, BUT IS STILL IMPORTANT TO THE TONE OF THE DRUM) FACING OUT TOWARD THE AUDIENCE.

YOU MAKE THE KICK DRUM SOUND BY PRESSING ON A BASS DRUM PEDAL WITH YOUR FOOT, (RIGHT FOOT FOR A RIGHTY AND LEFT FOOT FOR A LEFTY), WHICH MAKES THE "BEATER" SWING FORWARD AND HIT THE HEAD. (UNLESS, YOU ARE PLAYING DOUBLE BASS OR WITH A DOUBLE BASS DRUM PEDAL, IN WHICH CASE YOU USE BOTH FEET.)

THE KICK DRUM FOR ROCK IS USUALLY EITHER 22" OR 24", BUT COMES IN A RANGE OF SIZES FROM 18" TO 26" (JOHN BONHAM) AND EVEN LARGER FOR MARCHING BANDS.

STOMP ON THAT KICK PEDAL!

PUT A "BEATER PAD" ONTO THE BATTER SIDE OF THE BASS DRUM HEAD, EXACTLY WHERE THE BEATER MEETS THE HEAD, SO YOU CAN MAKE IT LAST LONGER.

PLAY THE BASS DRUM USING THE "HEEL-UP" POSITION.

HEEL-UP POSITION

Keith Moon

KEITH JOHN MOON WAS BORN ON AUGUST 23, 1946 IN WEMBLEY, MIDDLESEX, ENGLAND.

KEITH WAS HYPERACTIVE AND HAD A RESTLESS IMAGINATION WHEN HE WAS A BOY. MUSIC WAS THE ONE THING THAT COULD HOLD HIS ATTENTION.

ON HIS WAY HOME FROM SCHOOL KEITH WOULD GO TO "MACARI'S MUSIC STUDIO" ON EALING ROAD TO TAKE DRUM LESSONS AND PRACTICE ON THE DRUM SETS THERE. THIS IS WHERE HE LEARNED HIS BASIC DRUMMING SKILLS.

IN 1958, WHEN HE WAS 12, KEITH JOINED HIS LOCAL SEA CADET CORPS BAND AS A BUGLE PLAYER BUT TRADED HIS POSITION TO BE A DRUMMER.

IN 1960, WHEN HE WAS 14, KEITH'S FATHER BOUGHT HIM A DRUM SET. HE TOOK LESSONS FROM ONE OF THE LOUDEST DRUMMERS AT THE TIME, CARLO LITTLE.

MOON THE LOON

KEITH'S BIGGEST INFLUENCES WERE JAZZ ARTISTS **GENE KRUPA** AND **BUDDY RICH.**

IN 1963, WHEN HE WAS 17, KEITH JOINED "THE WHO." HE REPLACED THEIR ORIGINAL DRUMMER AFTER THE BAND WAS TOLD THAT THEY COULD NOT EXPECT A RECORDING CONTRACT WITHOUT A BETTER DRUMMER.

THROUGHOUT 1964 AND 1965 KEITH PLAYED FOUR, THEN FIVE-PIECE DRUM SETS. IN JUNE 1966 HE MOVED TO A "PREMIER" DOUBLE-BASS KIT. THIS NEW SET OPENED UP HIS PLAYING – HE ABANDONED HIS HI-HAT CYMBALS ALMOST ENTIRELY AND STARTED BASING HIS GROOVES ON A DOUBLE BASS OSTINATO WITH EIGHTH NOTE FLAMS, AND A WALL OF WHITE NOISE CREATED BY RIDING A CRASH OR RIDE CYMBAL. ON TOP OF THIS HE PLAYED FILLS AND CYMBAL ACCENTS – WHICH BECAME HIS TRADEMARK.

KEITH WAS 19 WHEN THE WHO RELEASED THEIR DEBUT ALBUM, "MY GENERATION," IN 1965.

THE SNARE DRUM

THE SNARE DRUM CREATES THE "BACK BEAT" OF THE DRUM PATTERN. IT IS WHAT PUSHES THE RHYTHM. IT IS THE HIGH SOUND THAT MAKES PEOPLE WANT TO MOVE, SHAKE, AND DANCE ... OR HEADBANG IN THE CASE OF HARD ROCK AND METAL!

THE SNARE DRUM IS THE HEART OF YOUR DRUM KIT. IT IS THE KICK DRUM'S PARTNER IN THE BEAT AND IS HIT THE MOST OUT OF ALL THE DRUMS (WHICH MEANS YOU WILL BE CHANGING THIS DRUM HEAD THE MOST!) IF THE KICK DRUM IS HIT ON THE 1 AND 3 OF THE DRUM BEAT COUNT, THEN THE SNARE IS HIT ON THE 2 AND 4. MOST DRUM FILLS USE THE SNARE, OR SNARE AND TOMS, IN COMBINATION.

THE SNARE IS SET UP BETWEEN THE DRUMMER'S LEGS ON A SNARE STAND WITH THE BATTER SIDE FACING UP AND THE RESONANT SIDE FACING DOWN. THE SNARE DRUM HAS METAL WIRES PUSHING UP AGAINST THE RESONANT (BOTTOM) HEAD, WHICH ARE CALLED A "SNARE STRAINER." THE STRAINER IS TIED TO THE "THROW OFF" WHICH CONTROLS WHETHER THE WIRES ARE UP AND TIGHT AGAINST THE RESONANT HEAD MAKING THE STANDARD SNARE DRUM SOUND, OR "OFF" WHICH MAKES THE SNARE DRUM SOUND LIKE A HIGH PITCHED TOM.

HIT THAT SNARE DRUM!

THE SNARE DRUM FOR ROCK IS USUALLY 5.5", 6.5", OR 7" DEEP AND 14" IN DIAMETER. IT COMES IN ALL TYPES OF METALS AND WOODS AND EACH HAS A DIFFERENT AND SIGNATURE SOUND. AGAIN, THE SNARE DRUM IS THE HEART OF THE DRUM KIT, SO IT IS A GOOD IDEA TO TRY OUT ALL THE DIFFERENT KINDS AND FIND ONE THAT SUITS YOUR STYLE AND SOUND.

ITS A GOOD IDEA TO INVEST IN A GOOD SNARE DRUM.

Bill Ward

WILLIAM THOMAS WARD WAS BORN ON MAY 5, 1948 IN ASTON, BIRMINGHAM, ENGLAND.

BILL BECAME INTERESTED IN DRUMMING WHEN HE WAS A TODDLER. WHEN HE WAS 3 YEARS OLD HE WOULD DRUM ON BOXES. WHEN HE WAS 7 HE GOT HIS FIRST DRUMS.

WHEN BILL WAS 11 HE GOT SERIOUS ABOUT PLAYING DRUMS.

BILL'S BIGGEST INFLUENCES ARE GENE KRUPA, BUDDY RICH, LOUIE BELLSON, LARRIE LONDON, BERNARD PURDIE, JOE MORELLO, KEIF HARTLEY, HUGHIE FLINT, JOHN BONHAM, RINGO STARR, JIM CAPALDI, AND CLIVE BUNKER.

BY THE TIME HE WAS 15 YEARS OLD BILL WAS PLAYING GIGS. HE PLAYED IN A BAND CALLED "THE REST" AND THEN A BAND CALLED "METHOD 5."

BILL MET TONY IOMMI IN 1964. BILL AND TONY FORMED A BAND CALLED "MYTHOLOGY."

IN 1967 BILL MET GEEZER BUTLER AT AN ALL NIGHT GIG. BILL SAYS, "GEEZER WAS BRILLIANT ON STAGE."

IN 1968 BILL MET OZZY AND THEY INSTANTLY BECAME FRIENDS.

BILL WAS 22 YEARS OLD WHEN BLACK SABBATH RECORDED THEIR FIRST ALBUM IN 1970.

THE BLACK SABBATH SONG "N.I.B." FROM THEIR FIRST ALBUM, WAS ALWAYS THOUGHT TO STAND FOR SOMETHING 'SINISTER.' HOWEVER, THE SONG'S TITLE SIMPLY REFERS TO BILL'S GOATEE THAT THE OTHER BAND MEMBERS REFERRED TO AS A "NIB."

THE TOMS

THE TOMS ARE USUALLY USED IN COMBINATION WITH THE KICK, SNARE, AND/OR CYMBALS TO PLAY DRUM FILLS.

THE TOMS ARE "TUNED" DRUMS THAT COME IN SIZES RANGING FROM 6"-18" IN DIAMETER. "RACK TOMS" ARE SET UP ON MOUNTS ATTACHED TO THE TOP OF THE BASS DRUM OR ON A SEPARATE FREE STANDING TOM STAND. "FLOOR TOMS" HAVE ADJUSTABLE LEGS ATTACHED TO THE DRUM THAT GO DOWN TO THE FLOOR.

"CONCERT TOMS" HAVE ONE HEAD ON THE BATTER SIDE AND "REGULAR" OR "POWER TOMS" HAVE BOTH BATTER AND RESONANT HEADS ON TOP AND BOTTOM.

SET-UP YOUR TOMS SO THE HEADS ARE BASICALLY LEVEL. THIS WAY YOUR STICK WILL HIT THE DRUMS AT A RELATIVELY FLAT ANGLE AND YOU WON'T DRIVE THE TIP OF THE STICK INTO THE HEAD. YOUR DRUMHEADS WILL LAST A LOT LONGER LIKE THIS. MOST OF THE PROS HAVE THEIR DRUMS FLAT.

TOMS PLACED WITH HEADS BASICALLY LEVEL >

HIT THE DRUM IN THE CENTER OF THE HEAD. THE FULLEST, DEEPEST TONE COMES FROM HITTING THE CENTER OF THE HEAD. WHEN YOU HIT THE DRUM CLOSE TO THE EDGE THE TONE GETS THINNER AND HIGHER.

THE AMOUNT OF TOMS YOU HAVE ON YOUR KIT DEPENDS ON WHAT YOU FEEL YOU NEED TO EXPRESS YOURSELF AND HOW MUCH MONEY YOU WANT TO SPEND! JOHN BONHAM PLAYED A 5-PIECE KIT WITH 1 RACK TOM AND 2 FLOOR TOMS ... NEIL PEART PLAYS AN 11-PIECE KIT WITH 5 RACK TOMS AND 3 FLOOR TOMS! IT'S ALL UP TO YOU!

THE CYMBALS

HI-HAT CYMBALS

THE HI-HATS ARE THE MOST PLAYED CYMBALS ON THE DRUM KIT BECAUSE YOU HIT THEM ALL THE TIME WHEN YOU PLAY A DRUM BEAT.

HI-HATS COME IN PAIRS WITH A TOP AND A BOTTOM CYMBAL. THEY ARE USUALLY 14" IN DIAMETER BUT ALSO COME SMALLER (13") OR LARGER (15") DEPENDING ON WHAT SOUND YOU WANT.

HI-HAT CYMBALS ARE MOUNTED ON THE HI-HAT STAND, WITH THE TOP HAT SCREWED ONTO A "CLUTCH" AND THE BOTTOM HAT SITTING LOOSE ON THE STAND. THE HI-HAT STAND HAS A PEDAL THAT PULLS THE TOP HAT CLUTCH DOWN WHEN PRESSED WITH YOUR FOOT. WHEN PUSHED DOWN YOU GET A CLOSED, "TIGHT" SOUND WHEN HIT WITH A STICK. WHEN PUSHED LIGHTLY OR NOT AT ALL YOU GET AN OPEN, LOUD SOUND. AND WHEN YOU PRESS DOWN WITH YOUR FOOT AND DON'T HIT THE HAT AT ALL, YOU GET A "CHICK" SOUND THAT IS USED OFTEN TO KEEP TIME IN THE BEAT WITHOUT USING YOUR HANDS.

RIDE CYMBALS

THE RIDE CYMBAL IS A LARGE CYMBAL THAT COMES IN SIZES RANGING FROM 20" TO 24" AND IS USUALLY PLAYED DURING THE CHORUS OR "SING ALONG" PART OF THE SONG.

A — BOW

IF THERE WAS A COIN WITH THE HI-HATS ON ONE SIDE, THEN THE RIDE WOULD BE ON THE OTHER SIDE, BECAUSE IF YOU'RE NOT PLAYING THE HI-HATS THEN CHANCES ARE YOU'RE PLAYING THE RIDE.

B — BELL

A) RIDE THE **BOW** WITH THE **TIP** OF YOUR STICK.

B) RIDE THE **BELL** WITH THE **SHOULDER** OF YOUR STICK.

CRASH CYMBALS

CRASH CYMBALS ARE THE CYMBALS YOU USE WHEN YOU WANT TO ACCENT THE BEGINNING OR END OF A MUSICAL PHRASE IN A SONG.

YOU USUALLY HIT THE CRASH AND KICK DRUM TOGETHER AT THE SAME TIME TO MAKE THIS ACCENT, BUT YOU CAN ALSO HIT THE SNARE OR TOM TOGETHER WITH THE CRASH.

THE CRASH CYMBAL SOUNDS BEST WHEN YOU HIT IT ON THE EDGE WITH THE SHOULDER OF YOUR STICK.

DO NOT HIT THE "BOW" OF THE CRASH WITH THE SHOULDER OF YOUR STICK. YOU WILL CRACK YOUR NICE, NEW CYMBAL.

CRASH CYMBALS COME IN SIZES FROM 16" TO 20".

CRASH GOOD

CRASH BAD

EFFECT CYMBALS

SPLASH CYMBALS ARE SMALL (8" – 14") CYMBALS USED FOR A QUICK ACCENT. THEY HAVE A FAST, SOFT, WATERY, "SPLASH" SOUND.

CHINA CYMBALS ARE CYMBALS THAT ARE ALSO USED FOR A QUICK ACCENT. THEY HAVE A ROUGH, TRASHY, CLANGY SOUND. CHINA CYMBALS HAVE AN UP-TURNED OUTER EDGE AND ARE MOUNTED UPSIDE DOWN.

THE HARDWARE

DON'T OVER TIGHTEN YOUR STANDS OR THEY WILL GET STRIPPED.

BASS DRUM PEDAL

A-K-A KICK PEDALS. WHEN YOU PRESS ON "THE FOOTBOARD" WITH YOUR FOOT, THE BEATER PUSHES FORWARD FROM TENSION ON AN ADJUSTABLE SPRING.

WHAT MAKES THEM FEEL AND SOUND DIFFERENT ARE THE BEATERS (FELT, PLASTIC, WOOD) AND WHAT CONNECTS THE FOOTBOARD TO THE PEDAL (FABRIC STRAPS, CHAINS, DIRECT DRIVE). TRY THEM ALL OUT AND DECIDE WHICH WORKS BEST FOR YOU.

APPLY PRESSURE TO THE PEDAL WITH JUST THE BALL OF YOUR FOOT.

PLAY THE BASS DRUM WITH THE HEEL —UP FOR **SPEED, POWER, AND ENDURANCE.**

HI-HAT STAND

PLAY THE HI-HATS USING BOTH HEEL-UP OR HEEL-DOWN DEPENDING ON THE SITUATION.

HEEL —UP POSITION

HEEL —DOWN POSITION

WHEN YOU PLAY THE HI-HATS WITH YOUR STICKS YOU WANT YOUR HEEL-DOWN.

SNARE STAND

ADJUST THE ANGLE OF STAND SO THE SNARE DRUM IS AS FLAT AS POSSIBLE. ADJUST THE HEIGHT OF THE STAND SO YOU CAN EASILY PLAY BOTH OPEN STROKES AND RIM-SHOTS.

RIM-SHOT

RIM-SHOT – STRIKE THE RIM AT THE SAME TIME THAT YOU HIT THE HEAD. HIT THE CENTER OF THE DRUM HEAD WHEN YOU DO A RIM-SHOT. BECAUSE THE SHELL VIBRATES MORE, THE RIM-SHOT ADDS DEPTH TO YOUR DRUM'S TONE.

CYMBAL STANDS

CYMBAL STANDS ARE THE SAME EXCEPT FOR BEING LIGHT, MEDIUM, OR HEAVY DUTY. PUT YOUR CRASH CYMBALS ON THE MOST HEAVY-DUTY STANDS POSSIBLE.

DON'T OVER TIGHTEN THE WING NUTS ON THE TOP OF YOUR CYMBAL STANDS OR YOU WILL "CHOKE" THE CYMBAL. THE CYMBALS NEED ROOM TO VIBRATE.

THE THRONE

PLACE THE DRUM THRONE (SEAT) SO THAT WHEN YOU SIT ON IT AND PUT YOUR FEET ON THE BASS PEDAL AND THE HI-HAT PEDAL, YOUR ANKLE IS RIGHT BELOW YOUR KNEE. YOUR KNEE SHOULD MAKE A 90 DEGREE ANGLE. THIS WILL GIVE YOU THE MOST SPEED, POWER, AND ENDURANCE.

THE STICKS

THE STICKS COME IN WOOD OR PLASTIC, HAVE DIFFERENT LENGTHS, THICKNESSES, AND TIPS. THE TIPS COME IN EITHER WOOD OR NYLON. IT'S UP TO THE DRUMMER TO TRY OUT THE DIFFERENT TYPES AND SIZES TO DECIDE WHICH FEELS AND WORKS THE BEST FOR THEIR STYLE.

TYPE OF WOOD – HICKORY IS A COMMON, WELL–ROUNDED WOOD WITH GOOD FLEX AND ENERGY ABSORPTION (SO YOU FEEL LESS OF THE HIT IN YOUR HANDS). MAPLE IS SOFTER THAN HICKORY AND OAK IS HARDER.

SIZE – THE MOST COMMON SIZE FOR ROCK IS THE 5B. THESE ARE THICKER THAN AVERAGE. THEY ALLOW FOR LOUDER SOUNDING DRUMS, AND ARE IDEAL FOR HEAVY ROCK AND METAL.

TIP – WOOD TIPPED DRUMSTICKS ARE THE MOST COMMON. BUT WOOD TIPS CHIP AFTER HEAVY USE AND CAN SPLINTER AND DAMAGE YOUR DRUM HEADS!

NYLON TIP STICKS GIVE A SLIGHTLY WARMER SOUND, ARE GREAT FOR BRINGING OUT YOUR CYMBALS, AND GETTING BETTER REBOUND FROM YOUR STICK. THE NYLON TIP PROTECTS THE DRUM HEAD FROM SPLINTERING WOOD.

BREAKIN' STICKS IS THE COST OF DOIN' BUSINESS!

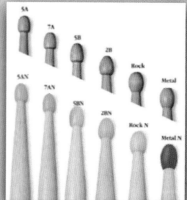

THE GRIPS

HOW TO HOLD THE STICKS

THERE ARE TWO DIFFERENT STYLES OF HOLDING THE STICKS, THE *"TRADITIONAL GRIP"* AND THE *"MATCHED GRIP."*

MATCHED GRIP

YOU HOLD BOTH STICKS THE SAME WAY WITH THE MATCHED GRIP. BOTH OF YOUR HANDS HOLD THE STICK LIKE A BASEBALL BAT.

MATCHED GRIP IS THE MOST COMMON GRIP USED TODAY. IT IS EASIER TO GET AROUND THE KIT AND YOU CAN HIT HARDER WITH THIS GRIP.

KEEP A *"TIGHTLY LOOSE"* GRIP. LET THE STICK BOUNCE AFTER THE HIT.

THE RIGHT-HAND GRIP IS THE SAME FOR BOTH THE MATCHED GRIP AND THE TRADITIONAL GRIP. IT'S THE LEFT-HAND GRIP THAT IS DIFFERENT WITH THE TRADITIONAL GRIP.

TRADITIONAL GRIP

THE **TRADITIONAL GRIP** IS MAINLY USED BY MARCHING BANDS AND JAZZ PLAYERS. IT COMES FROM MILITARY DRUMMERS WHO HELD THE DRUM ON A STRAP OVER THEIR SHOULDER WITH THE DRUM TILTED AT AN ANGLE. THEY HAD TO USE A DIFFERENT GRIP WITH THEIR LEFT HAND TO HIT THE DRUM WITH FORCE.

RHYTHM NOTATION

THE TIME VALUE IS DETERMINED BY THREE THINGS...

1) NOTE HEAD   **2) STEM**   **3) FLAG**

 THIS IS A **WHOLE NOTE**. THE NOTE HEAD IS OPEN AND HAS NO STEM. IN 4/4 TIME, A WHOLE NOTE RECEIVES 4 COUNTS.

 THIS IS A **HALF NOTE**. IT HAS AN OPEN HEAD AND A STEM. IN 4/4 TIME, A HALF NOTE RECEIVES 2 COUNTS.

 THIS IS A **QUARTER NOTE**. IT HAS A SOLID NOTE HEAD AND A STEM. IN 4/4 TIME, A QUARTER NOTE RECEIVES 1 COUNT.

 THIS IS AN **8TH NOTE**. IT HAS A SOLID NOTE HEAD AND A STEM WITH A FLAG ATTACHED. IN 4/4 TIME, AN EIGHTH NOTE RECEIVES 1/2 COUNT.

 THIS IS AN **16TH NOTE**. IT HAS A SOLID NOTE HEAD AND A STEM WITH A FLAG ATTACHED. IN 4/4 TIME, AN EIGHTH NOTE RECEIVES 1/2 COUNT.

WHOLE NOTE
COUNT:

HALF NOTE
COUNT:

QUARTER NOTE
COUNT:

EIGHTH NOTE
COUNT:

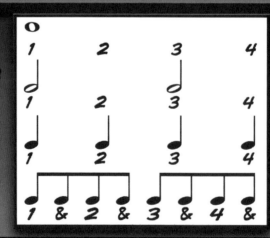

A **REST** IS USED TO INDICATE SILENCE IN MUSIC:

WHOLE REST   HALF REST   QUARTER REST   EIGHTH REST   SIXTEENTH REST

READING MUSIC FOR DRUMS

YES, YOU NEED TO LEARN TO READ MUSIC!!!!!!!!! READING MUSIC MAKES THE LEARNING PROCESS FASTER AND SPEEDS UP YOUR GROWTH RATE. READING MUSIC AND UNDERSTANDING NOTE VALUES AND MUSICAL TERMS HELPS YOU COMMUNICATE WITH OTHER MUSICIANS. READING MUSIC ENABLES YOU TO TRANSCRIBE BEATS, FILLS, AND PHRASES. I MEAN C'MON, IT'S NOT THAT HARD IF YOU PRACTICE JUST A LITTLE.

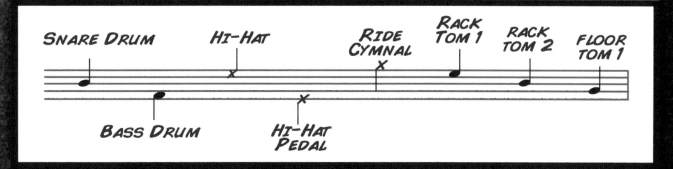

23

Neil Peart

NEIL ELLWOOD PEART WAS BORN ON SEPTEMBER 12, 1952 IN HAMILTON, ONTARIO, CANADA.

WHEN NEIL WAS BOY HE WOULD DRUM ON THINGS AROUND THE HOUSE WITH A PAIR OF CHOPSTICKS. FOR HIS 13TH BIRTHDAY HIS PARENTS BOUGHT HIM A PAIR OF DRUM STICKS, A PRACTICE DRUM, AND SOME LESSONS, WITH THE PROMISE THAT IF HE STUCK WITH IT, THEY WOULD BUY HIM A DRUM SET.

IN 1966 HIS PARENTS BOUGHT HIM A DRUM SET FOR HIS 14TH BIRTHDAY. HE CONTINUED TAKING LESSONS.

NEIL PLAYED AT LAKEPORT HIGH SCHOOL WITH HIS FIRST GROUP, "THE ETERNAL TRIANGLE." HE PERFORMED HIS FIRST DRUM SOLO AT THAT SHOW.

NEIL'S BIGGEST INFLUENCES WERE KEITH MOON AND JOHN BONHAM.

IN HIS TEENS, NEIL PLAYED IN SEVERAL LOCAL BANDS.

IN 1970, WHEN HE WAS 18, NEIL TRAVELLED TO LONDON, ENGLAND WITH THE HOPES OF BECOMING A PROFESSIONAL MUSICIAN. HE PLAYED IN SEVERAL BANDS AND DID SOME SESSION WORK BUT IT DIDN'T WORK OUT AND IN 1972 NEIL RETURNED HOME TO CANADA.

AFTER RETURNING TO CANADA, NEIL PLAYED IN A BAND CALLED "HUSH." IN 1974, WHEN HE WAS 22 YEARS OLD, NEIL AUDITIONED FOR THE TORONTO-BASED BAND "RUSH," WHO WERE LOOKING FOR A REPLACEMENT FOR THEIR ORIGINAL DRUMMER.

NEIL OFFICIALLY JOINED RUSH ON JULY 29, 1974, TWO WEEKS BEFORE THE GROUP'S FIRST US TOUR OPENING FOR URIAH HEEP AND MANFRED MANN.

NEIL'S FIRST RECORDING WITH RUSH, "FLY BY NIGHT," WAS RELEASED IN 1975.

TIME SIGNITURES

AT THE BEGINNING OF EVERY SONG IS A "TIME SIGNITURE."

THERE ARE TWO NUMBERS THAT MAKE UP A TIME SIGNITURE. THE TOP NUMBER TELLS YOU HOW MANY BEATS THERE ARE IN EACH MEASURE. THE BOTTOM NUMBER TELLS YOU WHAT NOTE VALUE RECEIVES THAT BEAT. (1/4 NOTE OR 1/8 NOTE.)

TIME SIGNITURE

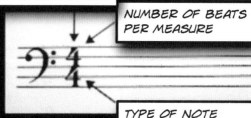

NUMBER OF BEATS PER MEASURE

TYPE OF NOTE RECEIVING ONE BEAT

YOU ARE THE TIME KEEPER!

SOMETIMES YOU WILL SEE 4/4 WRITTEN AS "C." THIS STANDS FOR "COMMON TIME."

COMMON TIME

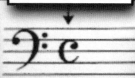

FOUR (4) BEATS PER MEASURE, QUARTER NOTE (1/4) EQUALS ONE BEAT

THREE (3) BEATS PER MEASURE, QUARTER NOTE (1/4) EQUALS ONE BEAT

SIX (6) BEATS PER MEASURE, EIGHTH NOTE (1/8) EQUALS ONE BEAT

THE MOST COMMON TIME SIGNITURES ARE 4/4 (COMMON TIME), 2/4 (CUT TIME), AND 3/4.

GO TO WWW.THEROCKMONSTERS.COM/DRUMS FOR VIDEO EXAMPLES.

TOMMY ALDRIDGE

TOMMY ALDRIDGE WAS BORN ON AUGUST 15, 1950 IN PEARL, MISSISSIPPI.

TOMMY TAUGHT HIMSELF TO PLAY THE DRUMS. HE WAS INSPIRED TO PLAY DRUMS AFTER HEARING CREAM, THE BEATLES, JIMI HENDRIX, AND LED ZEPPELIN. DRUMMERS JOE MORELLO AND JOHN BONHAM WERE ESPECIALLY INFLUENTIAL.

IN 1972 TOMMY JOINED UP AND COMING ROCKERS "BLACK OAK ARKANSAS." BETWEEN 1972 AND 1976 TOMMY RECORDED NINE ALBUMS WITH THEM AND TOURED CONSTANTLY THROUGHOUT THE UNITED STATES.

IN 1978 TOMMY JOINED "THE PAT TRAVERS BAND." TOMMY RECORDED FIVE ALBUMS WITH THE CANADIAN BLUES-ROCK GUITARIST AND TOURED CONSTANTLY WITH HIM.

IN 1980 TOMMY WAS OFFERED A PLACE IN OZZY OSBOURNE'S TOURING BAND, WHICH HE ACCEPTED BECAUSE OF THE TALENT OF RANDY RHOADS. TOMMY SAID IT WAS RANDY WHO PUSHED HIM TO BE THE BEST HE COULD BE.

TOMMY'S LAST PERFORMANCE PLAYING WITH OZZY WAS AT BRAZIL'S "ROCK IN RIO" MUSIC FESTIVAL IN EARLY 1985. QUEEN, SCORPIONS, AND WHITESNAKE ALSO PLAYED AT THAT SHOW.

TOMMY JOINED FORCES WITH LONGTIME FRIEND AND BASS PLAYER RUDY SARZO AND GUITAR/KEYBOARD VIRTUOSO TONY MACALPINE TO FORM M.A.R.S.

IN 1987, FOLLOWING THE RELEASE OF THE ALBUM "WHITESNAKE," DAVID COVERDALE HIRED TOMMY AND RUDY SARZO TO JOIN WHITESNAKE AND THEY WERE PART OF THAT BAND AT THE PEAK OF ITS SUCCESS. THEY TOURED TO SOLD OUT CROWDS FOR THE NEXT TWO YEARS SUPPORTING THE 1987 ALBUM .

TOMMY APPEARED ON WHITESNAKE'S 1989 ALBUM, "SLIP OF THE TONGUE." WHITESNAKE REMAINED MASSIVELY SUCCESSFUL AND TOURED THE WORLD TO SUPPORT THE ALBUM. THEY CO-HEADLINED THE 1990 "MONSTERS OF ROCK" FESTIVAL AT DONNINGTON PARK IN ENGLAND WITH AEROSMITH.

TOMMY IS A VERY INFLUENTIAL DRUMMER, REGARDED AS A DOUBLE BASS PIONEER.

THE RUDIMENTS

THE RUDIMENTS ARE THE FOUNDATION OF ALL DRUMMING. MILITARY DRUMMERS USED THE RUDIMENTS TO SEND MESSAGES TO THE TROOPS AND SIGNAL MANEUVERS ON THE BATTLEFIELD.

THE RUDIMENTS WERE "CODIFIED" IN 1869 BY GARDINER A. STRUBE, A DRUM MAJOR IN THE ARMY. HE WROTE A BOOK WITH THE 26 MOST POPULAR AND USEFUL PATTERNS HE LEARNED WHILE SERVING IN THE ARMY. ON APRIL 17TH, 1869, HIS BOOK, "THE STRUBES DRUM AND FIFE INSTRUCTOR," WAS ADOPTED BY THE U.S. ARMY AS THE MANUAL FOR TRAINING MILITARY FIELD MUSICIANS.

SINCE THEN, PRACTICING THE 26 STANDARD RUDIMENTS FOUND IN HIS BOOK HAS BEEN THE BEST METHOD FOR DRUMMERS OF ALL STYLES TO DEVELOP HAND-TO-HAND COORDINATION. FLUENCY WITH THESE STICKING PATTERNS HELPS YOU TO CREATE A RELAXED SOUND.

LEARN TO PLAY 'EM ALL!

THE BASIC RUDIMENTS:
1. THE SINGLE-STROKE ROLL
2. THE DOUBLE-STROKE ROLL
3. THE PARADIDDLE
4. THE FLAM
5. THE RUFF

THE RUDIMENTS

ALL THESE EXAMPLES ARE WRITTEN TO BE PLAYED ON THE SNARE DRUM.

SINGLE STROKE ROLL

R L R L

DOUBLE STROKE ROLL

R R L L

FIVE STROKE ROLL

R R L L R   R   R L L R
L L R R L

A GOOD WAY TO THE PRACTICE THE RUDIMENTS IS TO SET YOUR METRONOME AT A MODERATE TEMPO AND PLAY THE EXERCISE STEADILY FOR A FEW MINUTES.

SEVEN STROKE ROLL

R R L L R R L   L   R L R L
L L R R L L R

OR START OUT SLOWLY AND BUILD UP SPEED UNTIL YOU HIT THE FASTEST THAT YOU CAN PLAY AND STILL BE IN CONTROL. HOLD THAT TEMPO AND THEN SLOWLY REDUCE YOUR SPEED UNTIL YOU'RE BACK WHERE YOU BEGAN.

NINE STROKE ROLL

R R L L R R L L R
L L R R L L L R R L

TEN STROKE ROLL

L L R R L L L R R L   R
R R L L R R L L L R   L

FLAM

LR RL LR RL

FLAM ACCENT

L R L R R L R L

FLAM PARADIDDLE

L R L R R RL R L L

FLAM TAP

LR R RL L

SINGLE PARADIDDLE

R L R R L R L L

RUFF

LLR RRL

DOUBLE PARADIDDLE

R L R L R R L R L R L L

DOUBLE RATAMACUE

LLR LLRLRL
RRL RRLRLR

FLAM PARADIDDLEDIDDLE

LR L R R L L R L R L L R R

PHIL RUDD

PHILLIP HUGH NORMAN WITSCHKE RUDZEVECUIS WAS BORN ON MAY 19, 1954 IN MELBOURNE, AUSTRALIA.

PHIL BEGAN PLAYING DRUMS IN HIS TEENS AND WAS SERIOUS ABOUT PURSUING A CAREER IN MUSIC.

PHIL PLAYED IN SEVERAL BANDS IN MELBOURNE BEFORE JOINING A BAND CALLED "BUSTER BROWN" WITH FUTURE "ROSE TATTOO" VOCALIST ANGRY ANDERSON. BUSTER BROWN RELEASED ONE ALBUM, "SOMETHING TO SAY," IN 1974.

IN 1974 PHIL HEARD THAT AC/DC WAS AUDITIONING DRUMMERS. PHIL AUDITIONED AND WAS HIRED IMMEDIATELY.

PHIL'S DRUMMING STYLE SUITED MALCOLM AND ANGUS YOUNG'S STYLE OF MUSIC. PHIL BECAME AN INTEGRAL PART OF AC/DC'S SOUND FROM 1975 TO 1983.

PHIL WAS VERY GOOD FRIENDS WITH BON SCOTT. WHEN BON DIED PHIL TOOK IT BADLY. PHIL CONTINUED ON WITH AC/DC UNTIL 1983, BUT HE LEFT THE BAND DURING THE RECORDING OF THE "FLICK OF THE SWITCH" ALBUM.

AFTER LEAVING AC/DC, PHIL LIVED IN NEW ZEALAND WHERE HE RACED CARS, FLEW HELICOPTERS, BECAME A FARMER, AND SPENT TIME WITH HIS FAMILY. PHIL CONTINUED TO PLAY DRUMS AND BUILT HIS OWN RECORDING STUDIO.

WHEN AC/DC TOURED NEW ZEALAND IN 1991 IN SUPPORT OF THEIR RAZORS EDGE ALBUM, THEY CALLED PHIL TO SEE IF HE WOULD BE INTERESTED IN A JAM SESSION. PHIL ACCEPTED THEIR OFFER. PHIL WAS INVITED TO REJOIN AC/DC IN LATE 1993.

AC/DC WELCOMED PHIL BACK MAINTAINING THAT A CERTAIN GROOVE HAD BEEN MISSING FROM AC/DC'S MUSIC SINCE PHIL'S DEPARTURE IN 1983.

IN 2003, HE WAS INDUCTED INTO THE ROCK AND ROLL HALL OF FAME ALONG WITH THE OTHER MEMBERS OF AC/DC.

THE BASIC BEATS

THE KEY TO PLAYING THE BASIC BEATS IS TO CREATE A TIGHT, HARD-DRIVING FEEL. THE BACKBEAT SHOULD BE STRONG, THE BASS DRUM SOLID, AND THE HI-HAT SMOOTH.

THE BACKBEAT

THE BACKBEAT IS THE FOUNDATION OF ALL ROCK DRUMMING. IT IS THE DRIVING RHYTHM YOU HEAR IN MOST POP AND ROCK MUSIC THAT MAKES YOU WANT TO DANCE.

THE SNARE DRUM CREATES THE BACKBEAT. PLAY THE SNARE ON THE SECOND AND FOURTH BEATS OF THE MEASURE.

PLAY THE BACKBEAT WITH AUTHORITY. HIT THE SNARE DRUM SOLIDLY IN THE CENTER OF THE HEAD TO MAKE A DEEP, FULL TONE.

PLAY RIM-SHOTS TO ADD DEPTH TO YOUR DRUM'S SOUND. YOU DON'T NEED TO PLAY LOUD TO GET A STRONG TONE WITH RIM-SHOTS .

8TH NOTE FEEL

MOST ROCK MUSIC IS PLAYED WITH AN **EIGHTH-NOTE FEEL**. TYPICALLY THE MUSIC IS IN 4/4 TIME AND YOU PLAY EIGHTH NOTES ON THE HI-HATS OR THE RIDE CYMBAL.

PLAY THE SNARE DRUM ON THE SECOND AND FOURTH BEATS OF THE MEASURE. PLAY THE BASS DRUM ON THE FIRST AND THIRD BEATS OF THE MEASURE.

ALEX VAN HALEN

ALEXANDER ARTHUR VAN HALEN WAS BORN ON MAY 8, 1953 IN AMSTERDAM, NETHERLANDS.

ALEX'S FATHER WAS A PROFESSIONAL JAZZ CLARINET PLAYER. BOTH ALEX AND AND HIS LITTLE BROTHER EDDIE TOOK YEARS OF CLASSICAL PIANO LESSONS WHEN THEY WERE YOUNG.

THE VAN HALEN FAMILY MOVED TO PASADENA, CALIFORNIA IN 1962 WHEN ALEX WAS 9 YEARS OLD.

WHEN ALEX WAS 12 HE BEGAN TO TAKE GUITAR LESSONS AND EDDIE BEGAN TO LEARN TO PLAY THE DRUMS. WHEN EDDIE WAS OUT, ALEX WOULD PLAY HIS BROTHER'S DRUMS. WHEN EDDIE SAW HOW GOOD ALEX WAS ON THE DRUMS, ED DECIDED TO LEARN TO PLAY GUITAR.

ALEX AND EDDIE FORMED THEIR FIRST BAND, "THE BROKEN COMBS," WHEN THEY WERE IN GRADE SCHOOL. IT WAS AT THIS TIME THAT AL AND ED STARTED TO WANT TO BECOME PROFESSIONAL MUSICIANS.

ALEX'S BIGGEST INFLUENCES WERE JOHN BONHAM, GINGER BAKER, BUDDY RICH, KEITH MOON AND BUDGIE DRUMMER, RAY PHILLIPS.

WHILE HE WAS IN HIGH SCHOOL ALEX WORKED ALMOST EVERY WEEKEND PLAYING DRUMS IN HIS DAD'S WEDDING BAND.

IN 1971, ALEX GRADUATED FROM HIGH SCHOOL. HE THEN TOOK CLASSES IN MUSIC THEORY, SCORING, COMPOSITION AND ARRANGING AT PASADENA CITY COLLEGE.

IN 1972 ALEX MET MICHAEL ANTHONY AND DAVID LEE ROTH AT THE COLLEGE. DAVE AND MIKE JOINED THE VAN HALEN BROTHERS IN THEIR BAND "MAMMOTH."

IN 1974 THEY CHANGED THEIR NAME TO "VAN HALEN." IN ADDITION TO HIS MUSICAL DUTIES, AL HANDLED MANAGERIAL DUTIES, SUCH AS BOOKING GIGS FOR THE BAND.

ALEX WAS 24 YEARS OLD WHEN VAN HALEN RECORDED THEIR FIRST ALBUM IN 1977.

16TH NOTE FEEL

THE SIXTEENTH-NOTE FEEL IS CREATED BY PLAYING SIXTEENTH NOTES ON THE HI-HAT OR RIDE CYMBAL.

PLAY THE SNARE DRUM ON THE SECOND AND FOURTH BEATS OF THE MEASURE.

SONGS WITH A SIXTEENTH-NOTE FEEL ARE USUALLY SLOWER THAN SONGS WITH AN EIGHTH-NOTE FEEL.

AT **SLOWER TEMPOS**, YOU PLAY THE HI-HAT WITH YOUR RIGHT-HAND AND THE SNARE WITH YOUR LEFT.

AT **FASTER TEMPOS** YOU PLAY THE HI-HAT WITH BOTH HANDS. YOUR RIGHT HAND ALTERNATES BETWEEN THE HI-HAT AND THE SNARE.

HALF-TIME FEEL

THE HALF-TIME FEEL IS CREATED BY PLAYING THE SNARE DRUM ONLY HALF AS OFTEN AS YOU WOULD WITH THE REGULAR-TIME FEEL. INSTEAD OF HITTING THE SNARE DRUM TWICE DURING THE MEASURE (ON THE SECOND AND FOURTH BEATS), HIT THE SNARE ONLY ONCE ON THE THIRD BEAT.

THE HALF-TIME FEEL GIVES A SONG THE FEELING OF BEING SLOWER (HALF AS FAST) THAN IT ACTUALLY IS.

USE THE HALF-TIME FEEL DURING VERSES OR QUIETER PARTS OF SONGS.

GO TO WWW.THEROCKMONSTERS.COM/DRUMS FOR VIDEO EXAMPLES.

THE BLUES

MOST ROCK N' ROLL AND CLASSIC ROCK IS BASED ON THE BLUES. BECAUSE IT IS THE BASIS FOR SO MUCH MUSIC, LEARNING THE BLUES IS AN IMPORTANT STEP IN LEARNING TO PLAY DRUMS.

THE BLUES HAS IT'S ORIGINS IN THE MUSICAL TRADITIONS OF THE WEST AFRICAN PEOPLE BROUGHT TO AMERICA AS SLAVES. THE **WORK SONGS, FIELD HOLLERS,** AND **SPIRITUALS** OF THE AFRICAN-AMERICAN COMMUNITIES IN THE SOUTHERN UNITED STATES EVENTUALLY EVOLVED INTO THE BLUES.

IN THE **1940'S** MANY AFRICAN-AMERICANS MOVED TO THE CITIES IN THE NORTH WHERE THERE WERE JOBS IN FACTORIES. THE BLUES MUSICIANS WHO MOVED NORTH STARTED USING ELECTRIC GUITARS AND DRUMS TO BE HEARD IN THE LOUD, CROWDED NIGHTCLUBS WHERE THEY PLAYED.

IN THE **1950'S** ROCK N' ROLL EVOLVED FROM THE BLUES. AS **MUDDY WATERS** SAID, "THE BLUES HAD A BABY, AND THEY NAMED THE BABY ROCK N' ROLL."

5 CLASSIC BLUES RIFFS
I'M A MAN – MUDDY WATERS
YOU SHOOK ME – MUDDY WATERS
HOOCHIE COOCHIE MAN – MUDDY WATERS
BOOM BOOM – JOHN LEE HOOKER
BORN UNDER A BAD SIGN – ALBERT KING

IN THE **1960'S** A SMALL GROUP OF YOUNG ENGLISH MUSICIANS GOT THEIR START PLAYING THE BLUES. THE ROLLING STONES, THE YARDBIRDS, LED ZEPPELIN, AND MANY OTHERS WERE DEEPLY INFLUENCED BY THE BLUES. THEY RECORDED COVERS OF BLUES SONGS AND EXPOSED YOUNG ROCK AUDIENCES TO THE BLUES.

12 BAR BLUES – THE MOST COMMON BLUES CHORD PROGRESSION IS THE 12 BAR BLUES. LEARN THE 12 BAR BLUES STRUCTURE AND WHEN YOU GET TOGETHER WITH OTHER MUSICIANS YOU CAN JAM THE BLUES.

34

THE SHUFFLE

MOST BLUES SONGS HAVE A TRIPLET FEEL AND ARE WRITTEN IN 4/4 OR 12/8 TIME. (NO MATTER HOW THEY ARE WRITTEN, THEY STILL SOUND THE SAME!)

INSTEAD OF PLAYING 8TH OR 16TH NOTES, YOU PLAY "BROKEN TRIPLETS" TO CREATE THE **"SHUFFLE FEEL."**

"BROKEN TRIPLETS" ARE WHEN YOU PLAY THE FIRST AND LAST NOTES OF THE TRIPLET AND REST (DON'T PLAY) ON THE SECOND NOTE OF THE TRIPLET.

PLAY THE SNARE DRUM ON THE SECOND AND FOURTH BEATS OF THE MEASURE.

PLAY A VARIETY OF RHYTHMS ON THE BASS DRUM WITH EMPHASIS ON THE FIRST AND THIRD BEATS OF THE MEASURE.

EXAMPLE 1

EXAMPLE 2

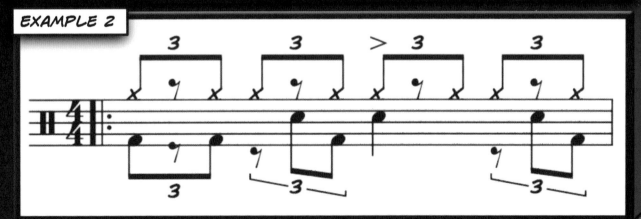

GO TO THEROCKMONSTERS.COM/DRUMS FOR VIDEO EXAMPLES.

TOMMY LEE

THOMAS LEE BASS WAS BORN ON OCTOBER 3, 1962 IN ATHENS, GREECE.

TOMMY IS THE SON OF DAVID OLIVER BASS, A US ARMY SERVICEMAN OF WELSH DESCENT, AND VASSILIKI PAPADIMITRIOU, A 1957 MISS GREECE CONTESTANT. HIS FAMILY MOVED TO WEST COVINA, CALIFORNIA ONE YEAR AFTER HE WAS BORN.

TOMMY GOT HIS FIRST DRUM WHEN HE WAS FOUR.
HE GOT HIS FIRST DRUM KIT WHEN HE WAS A TEENAGER.

TOMMY LISTENED TO QUEEN, KISS, DEEP PURPLE, LED ZEPPELIN AND JUDAS PRIEST. AFTER LISTENING TO KISS, HIS MAIN DRUM INFLUENCE BECAME PETER CRISS.

AFTER TRANSFERRING FROM SOUTH HILLS HIGH SCHOOL IN WEST COVINA, CA., HE JOINED THE MARCHING BAND AT ROYAL OAK HIGH SCHOOL IN COVINA, CALIFORNIA.

TOMMY'S FIRST SUCCESSFUL BAND, "SUITE 19," PLAYED THE SUNSET STRIP IN LOS ANGELES DURING THE LATE 1970'S. IT WAS DURING THIS TIME THAT HE MET FUTURE BANDMATE, NIKKI SIXX. CASUALLY, SIXX WAS FORMING A THEATRICAL BAND THAT WOULD SPECIALIZE IN ANTHEMIC HEAVY METAL, AND WAS IMPRESSED BY TOMMY'S DRUMMING.

AT THIS TIME, HE CHANGED HIS NAME TO "TOMMY LEE." SOON AFTERWARD, GUITARIST MICK MARS JOINED THE BAND. TOMMY RECOMMENDED HIS HIGH SCHOOL FRIEND, VINCE NEIL, TO SING VOCAL AND MÖTLEY CRÜE WAS FORMED.

MÖTLEY CRÜE QUICKLY BUILT A STRONG FAN BASE ON THE SUNSET STRIP IN HOLLYWOOD. IN 1981 THEY RELEASED "TOO FAST FOR LOVE" ON THEIR OWN INDEPENDENT LABEL. THE FIRST PRESSING OF THE RECORD SOLD OUT IN HOLLYWOOD, WHICH GOT THE ATTENTION OF THE RECORD COMPANIES. ELEKTRA RECORDS DECIDED TO SIGN THE BAND AND REISSUED "TOO FAST FOR LOVE" IN 1982.

TOMMY USED SEVERAL MEMORABLE GIMMICKS DURING HIS DRUM SOLOS AT CONCERTS, SUCH AS HAVING HIS ENTIRE KIT REVOLVING AND SPINNING, OR HAVING THE ENTIRE KIT FLOAT ABOVE THE CROWD WHILE HE CONTINUED TO PLAY. HE WAS LEGENDARY FOR MOONING THE CROWD AT NEARLY EVERY SHOW.

THE ROCK

REMEMBER, THE BACKBEAT IS THE BASIS OF ALL ROCK DRUMMING. THE SNARE DRUM CREATES THE BACKBEAT. HIT THE SNARE DRUM WITH AUTHORITY ON THE SECOND AND FOURTH BEATS OF THE MEASURE.

ROCK MUSIC IS USUALLY PLAYED WITH AN **EIGHTH-NOTE FEEL.** PLAY EIGHTH NOTES ON THE HI-HATS OR THE RIDE CYMBAL.

EXAMPLE 1

EXAMPLE 2

ROCK REQUIRES A STRONG, STEADY DRUMMER WHO CAN HOLD A DRIVING, POWERFUL BEAT. PRACTICE TO BUILD UP YOUR ENDURANCE.

EXAMPLE 3

SOME ROCK DRUMMING REQUIRES YOU TO PUSH THE BEAT. A LOT OF ROCK DRUMMING IS ALL ABOUT CREATING A HEAVY FEEL BY LAYING BACK A LITTLE. REMEMBER, THE SLOWER THE HEAVIER. MAKING IT FAST DOESN'T MAKE IT HARDER.

EXAMPLE 4

LISTEN TO AC/DC, AEROSMITH, THE ROLLING STONES, BAD CO. THE FACES, HUMBLE PIE, THIN LIZZY, LYNYRD SKYNYRD, MONTROSE, KISS, CHEAP TRICK, ZZ TOP ...

GO TO THEROCKMONSTERS.COM/DRUMS FOR VIDEO EXAMPLES.

MIKE BORDIN

MICHAEL ANDREW BORDIN WAS BORN ON NOVEMBER 27, 1962 IN SAN FRANCISCO, CALIFORNIA.

IN THE LATE 1970S, WHILE STILL IN HIGH SCHOOL, MIKE PLAYED IN THE BAND "EZ-STREET" WITH FUTURE METALLICA BASSIST CLIFF BURTON AND FUTURE FAITH NO MORE GUITARIST JIM MARTIN.

IN 1981, MIKE FORMED "FAITH NO MAN" WITH BASSIST BILLY GOULD, KEYBOARDIST WADE WORTHINGTON, AND FRONTMAN MIKE MORRIS.

A YEAR LATER THE GROUP CHANGED THEIR NAME TO "FAITH NO MORE." MIKE'S FORMER BANDMATE, JIM MARTIN, JOINED THE FOLLOWING YEAR AS GUITARIST.

FAITH NO MORE RELEASED THEIR FIRST ALBUM, "WE CARE A LOT," IN 1985.

AFTER RELEASING SEVERAL MORE ALBUMS, INCLUDING THE GRAMMY-NOMINATED "THE REAL THING," FAITH NO MORE DISBANDED IN 1998.

IN 1997, MIKE BEGAN PERFORMING WITH OZZY OSBOURNE'S BAND.

MIKE HAD A BRIEF STRETCH PLAYING WITH THE OTHER ORIGINAL MEMBERS OF BLACK SABBATH AFTER DRUMMER BILL WARD HAD HEALTH PROBLEMS WHILE ON TOUR. HE PLAYED THE CLOSING SEGMENTS OF OZZY OSBOURNE'S 1997 HEADLINING CONCERTS DURING THE OZZFEST TOUR.

AS A LEFT-HANDED DRUMMER, MIKE NOTABLY PLAYS WITH A RIGHT-HANDED KIT WITH HIS RIDE CYMBAL ON THE LEFT.

THE FUNK

THE MOST IMPORTANT THING IN FUNK IS **"THE GROOVE."** STEADY TIMEKEEPING IS CRUCIAL. FUNK IS ABOUT DANCING ~ "SHAKING YOUR BOOTY." AS THE DRUMMER, YOUR JOB IS TO MAKE AND KEEP THE BEAT FOR THE AUDIENCE TO DANCE TO.

FUNK IS ALL ABOUT PLAYING **"IN THE POCKET."** (SEE PAGE 7.) DON'T PUSH THE BEAT ~ LAY BACK AND PLAY IT COOL.

LISTEN TO JAMES BROWN, SLY AND THE FAMILY STONE, GRAHAM CENTRAL STATION, STEVIE WONDER, PARLIMENT FUNKADELIC, THE ISLEY BROTHERS, PRINCE... TO LEARN HOW TO PLAY FUNK.

EXAMPLE 1

EXAMPLE 2

GO TO THEROCKMONSTERS.COM/DRUMS FOR VIDEO EXAMPLES.

DAVE LOMBARDO

DAVID LOMBARDO WAS BORN ON FEBRUARY 16, 1965 IN HAVANA, CUBA.

WHEN DAVE WAS TWO YEARS OLD, HIS FAMILY MOVED TO SOUTH GATE, CALIFORNIA.

WHEN DAVE WAS IN THE THIRD GRADE, HE BROUGHT A SET OF BONGO DRUMS WITH A SANTANA RECORD TO SCHOOL FOR SHOW AND TELL AND PLAYED THE BONGOS ALONG WITH THE RECORD PERFECTLY.

DAVE'S FATHER SAW HIS SERIOUS INTEREST IN MUSIC AND WHEN DAVE WAS 10 HIS DAD BOUGHT HIM A FIVE-PIECE "MAXWIN" DRUM SET FOR $350.

DAVE BOUGHT HIS FIRST RECORD, "ALIVE!" BY KISS. HE TAUGHT HIMSELF TO PLAY THE DRUMS BY PLAYING ALONG TO THE RECORD OVER AND OVER. ESPECIALLY THE DRUM SOLO IN THE SONG "100,000 YEARS."

DAVE FORMED A BAND IN 1979 CALLED "ESCAPE," WITH TWO GUITARISTS. THE GROUP PERFORMED AC/DC, LED ZEPPELIN, AND BLACK SABBATH SONGS. THEY PLAYED AT PARTIES UNDER THE NAME "SABOTAGE."

WHEN DAVE WAS 16, HE MET GUITARIST KERRY KING, WHO LIVED CLOSE BY. DAVE ASKED KERRY IF HE WANTED TO JAM. THEY REHEARSED IN DAVE'S GARAGE SEVERAL TIMES. KERRY THEN INTRODUCED DAVE TO GUITARIST JEFF HANNEMAN. THE THREE REHEARSED A FEW MORE TIMES AND DECIDED THEY NEEDED A SINGER AND BASS PLAYER. KERRY HAD PLAYED WITH BASS PLAYER/SINGER TOM ARAYA IN A BAND AND DECIDED TO INTRODUCE DAVE AND JEFF TO TOM AND THUS FORMING THE ORIGINAL LINEUP OF "SLAYER."

SLAYER RELEASED THEIR FIRST ALBUM, "SHOW NO MERCY," IN 1983. THEY TOURED RELENTLESSLY FOR THE NEXT YEAR TO PROMOTE IT.

DAVE IS MOST WIDELY KNOWN AS A VERY AGGRESSIVE HEAVY METAL DRUMMER, AND HIS USE OF THE DRUMS HAVE BEEN CALLED "ASTONISHINGLY INNOVATIVE" AND EARNED HIM THE TITLE "THE GODFATHER OF DOUBLE BASS" FROM DRUMMER WORLD. OVER HIS CAREER, HE HAS HAD A SIGNIFICANT INFLUENCE ON THE METAL SCENE AND HAS INSPIRED MANY MODERN METAL DRUMMERS, PARTICULARLY WITHIN BOTH THRASH METAL AND DEATH METAL GENRES.

THE METAL

THE BLAST BEAT
USED FOR THRASH.

Ride Cym.
Snare
Bass

DOUBLE-BASS PATTERNS

SLOW

Hi-Hat
Snare
Dbl. Bass

FAST

Hi-Hat
Snare
Dbl. Bass

FASTER

Hi-Hat
Snare
Dbl. Bass

DON'T OVER USE THE DOUBLE-BASS!

WHEN PLAYING FAST METAL SONGS YOU WILL USUALLY BE **PUSHING** THE BEAT.

LISTEN TO SLAYER, MEGADETH, DEATH ANGEL, METALLICA, ... TO LEARN HOW TO PLAY METAL.

STEWART COPELAND

STEWART ARMSTRONG COPELAND WAS BORN ON JULY 16, 1952 IN ALEXANDRIA, VIRGINIA.

STEWART'S FATHER WAS A FOUNDING MEMBER OF THE "OFFICE OF STRATEGIC SERVICES" (OSS) AND THE "CENTRAL INTELLIGENCE AGENCY" (CIA).

DUE TO STEWART'S FATHER'S JOB, STEWART SPENT HIS EARLY YEARS LIVING IN THE MIDDLE EAST. STEWART'S FAMILY MOVED TO CAIRO, EGYPT A FEW MONTHS AFTER HE WAS BORN. IN 1957, WHEN STEWART WAS 5 YEARS OLD, HIS FAMILY MOVED TO BEIRUT, LEBANON.

STEWART STARTED TAKING DRUM LESSONS WHEN HE WAS 12. BY THE TIME HE WAS 13 YEARS OLD HE WAS PLAYING DRUMS AT SCHOOL DANCES.

IN 1967, WHEN STEWART WAS 15, HE MOVED TO ENGLAND TO ATTEND BOARDING SCHOOL.

IN 1970, WHEN STEWART WAS 18, HE MOVED TO CALIFORNIA TO GO TO COLLEGE AT U.C. BERKELEY.

IN 1974, WHEN STEWART WAS 22, HE MOVED BACK TO ENGLAND. HE WORKED AS THE ROAD MANAGER FOR THE PROGRESSIVE ROCK BAND "CURVED AIR." IN 1975 HE BECAME CURVED AIR'S DRUMMER.

IN 1977, WHEN HE WAS 25, STEWART FOUNDED "THE POLICE" WITH SINGER-BASSIST STING AND GUITARIST HENRY PADOVANI (WHO WAS REPLACED BY ANDY SUMMERS).

THE COMBINATION OF PUNK ROCK, REGGAE, AND JAZZ, ALONG WITH STEWART'S SYNCOPATED BEAT, MADE THE POLICE VERY UNIQUE.

STEWART WAS 26 YEARS OLD WHEN THE POLICE'S DEBUT ALBUM "OUTLANDOS D'AMOUR," AND THE SINGLE "ROXANNE" WAS RELEASED IN 1978.

DRUM FILLS

FILLS ARE USED TO TRANSITION FROM ONE PART OF A SONG TO ANOTHER. ADD A FILL WHEN YOU ARE GOING FROM THE VERSE TO THE CHORUS, OR FROM THE CHORUS BACK TO THE VERSE, OR GOING INTO THE BRIDGE (SEE "SONG STRUCTURE" ON PAGE 45.)

THE MOST IMPORTANT THING IS THAT YOU CAN'T LOSE OR GAIN TIME WHEN YOU DO A FILL. YOU MUST COME BACK IN ON TIME. MAKE SURE EACH HIT OF THE FILL IS ON THE BEAT OF THE TIMING YOU ARE IN (8THS OR 16THS.)

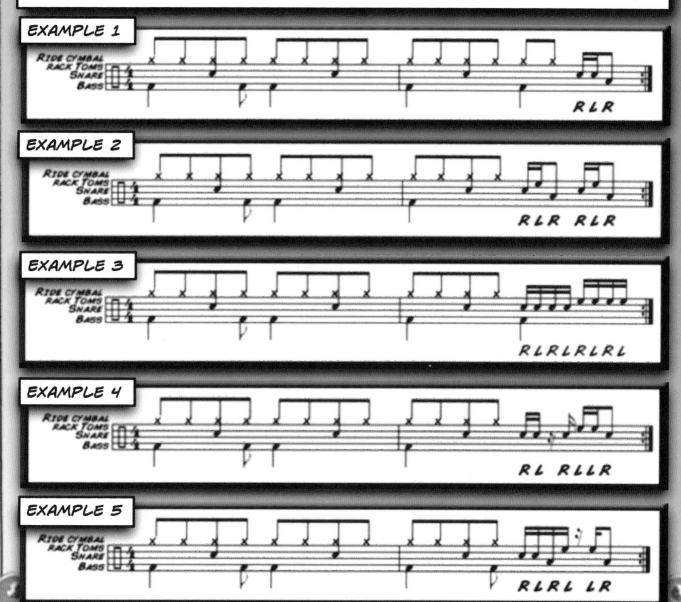

43

ANDREW GALEON WAS BORN ON MARCH 21, 1972 IN SAN FRANCISCO, CALIFORNIA.

WHEN HE WAS 8, ANDY AND HIS COUSINS WENT TO SEE "KISS" IN CONCERT AT THE COW PALACE IN 1979.

WHEN HE WAS 10, ANDY STARTED PLAYING IN A BAND WITH HIS COUSINS AFTER BEING INSPIRED TO PLAY BY THE KISS CONCERT.

"DEATH ANGEL" WAS FORMED IN THE SAN FRANCISCO BAY AREA IN 1982 BY COUSINS ROB CAVESTANY (LEAD GUITAR), DENNIS PEPA (VOCALS, BASS), GUS PEPA (RHYTHM GUITAR), AND ANDY (DRUMS).

ANDY'S BIGGEST INFLUENCES ARE EVERYONE IN THIS BOOK ... JOHN BONHAM, BILL WARD, PHILL RUDD, TOMMY ALDRIDGE, NEIL PEART, ALEX VAN HALEN, TOMMY LEE, DAVE LOMBARDO, MIKE BORDIN...

IN 1983 DEATH ANGEL RELEASED THEIR DEBUT DEMO "HEAVY METAL INSANITY."

WHILE ALL THE MEMBERS OF THE BAND WERE STILL IN HIGH SCHOOL, DEATH ANGEL PLAYED CLUB GIGS IN THE SAN FRANCISCO BAY AREA OPENING FOR BANDS LIKE W.A.S.P., MEGADETH, MERCYFUL FATE, ARMORED SAINT, AND METALLICA.

IN 1986, DEATH ANGEL RECORDED THE "KILL AS ONE" DEMO WITH METALLICA'S KIRK HAMMETT (WHOM THEY HAD MET AT A RECORD STORE SIGNING IN 1983) AS PRODUCER. THE TAPE TRADING SCENE OF THE EARLY 1980'S LED TO EXTENSIVE DISTRIBUTION OF THE DEMO, WHICH BROUGHT THE BAND TO THE ATTENTION OF A WIDE AUDIENCE.

THE SUCCESS OF "KILL AS ONE" LED TO A RECORD DEAL WITH ENIGMA RECORDS, WHO RELEASED DEATH ANGEL'S DEBUT ALBUM, "THE ULTRA-VIOLENCE," IN 1987. THE BAND RECORDED THE ALBUM WHEN ALL THE BAND MEMBERS WERE STILL UNDER 20 YEARS OLD. THE ALBUM SOLD 40,000 COPIES IN JUST FOUR MONTHS.

SONG STRUCTURE

IT IS IMPORTANT TO UNDERSTAND SONG STRUCTURE TO HELP YOU KNOW WHERE YOU ARE WITHIN THE SONG AND WHAT IS CALLED FOR WITH YOUR DRUM PARTS.

THE PARTS OF A SONG:

INTRO – A SHORT MUSICAL PHRASE AT THE BEGINNING OF THE SONG THAT IS USUALLY BETWEEN TWO AND EIGHT MEASURES (BARS) LONG.

VERSE – WHEN THE SINGING BEGINS THAT IS THE FIRST VERSE. VERSES ARE USUALLY EIGHT TO SIXTEEN BARS LONG. PLAY SOFTLY DURING THE VERSE SO THE VOCALS CAN BE HEARD AND YOU HAVE SOME ROOM TO BRING THE VOLUME UP FOR THE CHORUS. A FILL AND AN INCREASE IN VOLUME USUALLY MARKS THE TRANSITION FROM VERSE TO THE PRE-CHORUS OR CHORUS SECTION.

PRE-CHORUS – A PRE-CHORUS IS USED TO BUILD UP FROM THE VERSE TO THE CHORUS. IT IS USUALLY EIGHT TO SIXTEEN BARS LONG. (NOT ALL SONGS HAVE A PRE-CHORUS.)

CHORUS – THE CHORUS IS THE BIG PART OF THE SONG. IT IS LOUDER THAN THE VERSE AND USUALLY HAS THE **"HOOK"** – THE PART OF THE SONG YOU REMEMBER. THE CHORUS IS USUALLY EIGHT TO SIXTEEN BARS LONG. A FILL AND DECREASE IN VOLUME USUALLY MARKS THE TRANSITION FROM THE CHORUS BACK TO THE VERSE SECTION.

BRIDGE – THE BRIDGE IS A PART OF THE SONG THAT IS COMPLETELY DIFFERENT FROM ALL THE OTHER SECTIONS. IT USUALLY FOLLOWS THE SECOND OR THIRD CHORUS. IT IS BETWEEN FOUR TO SIXTEEN BARS LONG. THE BRIDGE IS SOMETIMES CALLED "THE MIDDLE EIGHT" BECAUSE IT IS EIGHT BARS IN THE MIDDLE OF THE SONG. (NOT ALL SONGS HAVE A BRIDGE.)

BREAKDOWN – DURING THE BREAKDOWN SECTION THE DRUMS AND BASS KEEP THE BEAT WHILE THE OTHER INSTRUMENTS DROP OUT. AFTER A FEW BARS THE VOCALS COME BACK IN. THE AUDIENCE CAN JOIN IN BY CLAPPING HANDS AND SINGING ALONG DURING THE BREAKDOWN. THE OTHER INSTRUMENTS CAN COME BACK IN ALL AT ONCE OR COME BACK IN SLOWLY TO BUILD UP TO A BIG CRESCENDO. (NOT ALL SONGS HAVE A BREAKDOWN.)

OUTRO – THE ENDING SECTION. MANY SONGS HAVE AN OUTRO GUITAR SOLO. THE OUTRO CAN LAST EIGHT, SIXTEEN, TWENTY-FOUR MEASURES ...

TYPICAL STRUCTURE FOR A ROCK SONG :
INTRO > 1ST VERSE > CHORUS > 2ND VERSE > CHORUS > BRIDGE > GUITAR SOLO > CHORUS (REPEAT 2X) > OUTRO...

TUNING DRUMS

ALL DRUMMERS MUST KNOW HOW TO TUNE THEIR DRUMS. NO MATTER HOW EXPENSIVE (OR INEXPENSIVE) YOUR DRUM SET IS, HOW YOU TUNE THE DRUMS HAS MORE IMPACT ON HOW GOOD THEY SOUND THAN WHAT KIND OF WOOD THEY ARE MADE OF OR WHAT KIND OF HARDWARE THEY HAVE.

THE KEY TO GETTING A GOOD TONE OUT OF A DRUM IS TUNING IT TO ITS **"SWEET SPOT".** THE SWEET SPOT IS THE PITCH WHERE THE DRUM RESONATES BEST. THE SWEET SPOT VARIES FROM DRUM TO DRUM DEPENDING ON THE SIZE OF THE DRUM, THE CONSTRUCTION OF THE SHELL, AND THE TYPE OF HEAD THAT YOU ARE USING.

TO FIND THE SWEET SPOT TIGHTEN EACH LUG ONE-QUARTER TO ONE-HALF A TURN UNTIL THE SOUND IS CLEAR AND WITHOUT A LOT OF OVERTONES. (OVERTONES ARE HIGHER PITCHED SOUNDS THAT THE DRUM CREATES.)

IF YOU NOTICE OVERTONES OR IF THE PITCH ISN'T REALLY CLEAR, LIGHTLY TAP THE HEAD WITH YOUR STICK ABOUT ONE INCH IN FROM EACH LUG. THE PITCHES SHOULD ALL BE THE SAME. ADJUST ANY THAT ARE OUT OF PITCH WITH THE OTHERS UNTIL ALL ARE THE SAME.

IF YOU'RE HAVING TROUBLE HEARING THE PITCH BECAUSE OF THE OVERTONES, PLACE YOUR FINGER AT THE CENTER OF THE DRUM WHILE TAPPING.

THE DRUM'S **PITCH** IS MOST AFFECTED BY HOW YOU TUNE THE BATTER (TOP) HEAD. A TIGHTER HEAD PRODUCES A HIGHER PITCH AND A LOOSER HEAD PRODUCES A LOWER PITCH. THE DRUM'S **TONE** AND RINGING IS MOST AFFECTED BY HOW YOU TUNE THE RESONANT (BOTTOM) HEAD.

SOME DRUMMERS TUNE BOTH THE BATTER HEAD AND THE RESONANT HEAD TO THE SAME PITCH. IF YOU TUNE THE HEADS TO THE SAME PITCH THEY WILL VIBRATE AT THE SAME FREQUENCY AND THE DRUM'S SOUND WILL RING AND LAST LONGER.

OTHER DRUMMERS TUNE THE RESONANT HEAD SLIGHTLY HIGHER OR LOWER THAN THE BATTER HEAD. IF YOU TUNE THE RESONANT HEAD TO A DIFFERENT PITCH, ITS VIBRATIONS WILL WORK AGAINST THE BATTER HEAD, DAMPEN THE SOUND, AND PRODUCE A FULLER DRUM SOUND.

MANY DRUMMERS PUT A PIECE OF DUCT TAPE ON THE BATTER HEAD OR TAPE A FOLDED UP PAPER TOWEL TO THE HEAD TO DAMPEN UNWANTED FREQUENCIES.

GO ACROSS THE DRUM AS YOU GO AROUND.

START WITH THE LUG AT THE TOP (12 O'CLOCK POSITION), THEN GO TO THE LUG AT THE SIX O'CLOCK POSITION. GO TO THE THREE O'CLOCK POSITION, THEN TO THE NINE O'CLOCK POSITION, AND SO FORTH UNTIL YOU GO ALL THE WAY AROUND. THIS METHOD ENSURES THAT YOU TUNE THE HEAD EVENLY ON ALL SIDES.

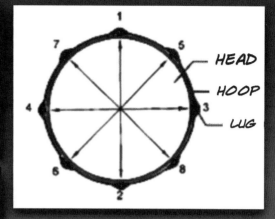

HEAD

HOOP

LUG

ONLY TIGHTEN EACH LUG ONE-QUARTER TO ONE-HALF A TURN.

CHECK THE DRUM'S PITCH (HOW HIGH OR LOW THE SOUND IS) BY HITTING THE DRUM IN THE CENTER OF THE HEAD WITH YOUR STICK.

CONTINUE GOING AROUND THE HEAD USING ONE-QUARTER TURNS UNTIL YOU GET TO A PITCH THAT RINGS FREELY.

TUNING THE SNARE DRUM

TUNE THE **SNARE DRUM** SO THAT IT SOUNDS HIGH PITCHED AND SNAPPY. TUNE THE BATTER HEAD TIGHTLY TO IMPROVE DRUMSTICK BOUNCE AND MAKE PLAYING EASIER. DISENGAGE THE SNARE WIRES WHEN TUNING A SNARE DRUM.

TUNING THE BASS DRUM

THE BASS DRUM PRODUCES BASS TONES EVEN WITH TIGHTLY TUNED HEADS. LOOSE HEADS PRODUCE UGLY SOUNDING OVERTONES.

TUNING THE BATTER HEAD AND RESONANT HEAD ON THE BASS DRUM TO DIFFERENT PITCHES HELPS MUFFLE RINGY OVERTONES AND PRODUCE A NICE, RING-LESS 'THUMP' SOUND. TRY TUNING THE RESONANT HEAD TIGHTLY (HIGHER PITCH TUNING), AND THE BATTER HEAD LOOSELY.

SOME DRUMMERS PUT A PILLOW, A TOWEL, OR SOME FOAM INSIDE THE BASS DRUM TO MUFFLE THE OVERTONES.

MAINTENANCE

DRUMS

EXPOSURE TO COLD, HEAT, DIRT, OR HUMIDITY (MOISTURE) CAN DAMAGE THE DRUM SHELL. IT WILL WARPING, AND CRACKING, AND RUST. DON'T LEAVE YOUR DRUMS OUTSIDE ALL DAY OR OVERNIGHT. DON'T STORE YOUR DRUMS WHERE THE TEMPERATURE IS TOO HOT OR TOO COLD OR TOO WET OR TOO DUSTY. (LIKE MOST GARAGES.)

IF YOU ARE GOING TO MOVE OR STORE YOUR DRUMS YOU NEED CASES OR BAGS. (IF NECESSARY, COVERING THE DRUM KIT WITH BLANKETS WILL WORK.) SLIGHTLY DETUNE THE HEADS IF YOU ARE GOING TO STORE THE DRUMS OR TRAVEL WITH THEM.

DUST OFF THE DRUMS WITH A SOFT CLOTH OR A FEATHER DUSTER. CLEAN ALL CHROME AND DRUM SHELLS WITH A MILD SOLUTION OF SOAPY WATER AND RUB UNTIL CLEAN. WIPE THE DRUMS WITH A MILD POLISH FOR A CLEAN SHINE.

CHANGE THE HEADS. OLD BRITTLE DRUM HEADS WILL FAIL TO DISPERSE THE PRESSURE EVENLY AND ULTIMATELY CAN CAUSE CRACKS IN THE WOOD OF YOUR DRUMS.

CYMBALS

HOLD CYMBALS BY THEIR EDGES ONLY. USE BOTH HANDS AT THE EDGE. THE OIL AND DIRT FROM YOUR HANDS IS NOT GOOD FOR YOUR CYMBALS. WIPE DOWN YOUR CYMBALS WITH A SOFT, DRY CLOTH AFTER EACH PRACTICE OR PERFORMANCE. CLEAN CYMBALS WITH WARM WATER AND MILD SOAP.

REST YOUR CYMBALS FLAT. AVOID STANDING CYMBALS ON THEIR EDGE ON HARD SURFACES SUCH AS CONCRETE FLOORS. ALWAYS PROTECT THE EDGE OF THE CYMBALS. NICKS AND DENTS INVARIABLY LEAD TO BREAKAGE.

IF YOU STACK CYMBALS FOR STORAGE, SEPARATE THEM FROM EACH OTHER WITH SOME SOFT MATERIAL OR PLASTIC. WHEN TRANSPORTING CYMBALS, ALWAYS USE A BAG OR A CASE. MAKE SURE CYMBALS CANNOT MOVE AROUND TOO MUCH AND ARE SEPARATED FROM EACH OTHER.

AVOID EXTREME COLD AND HEAT. LET YOUR CYMBALS ADJUST TO THE SURROUNDING TEMPERATURE BEFORE PLAYING THEM.

CHANGE YOUR CYMBAL SLEEVES. CYMBAL SLEEVES GET WORN DOWN AND CAN CAUSE THE RING OF YOUR CYMBAL TO CRACK.

CHANGING DRUM HEADS

1. **START BY REMOVING THE OLD DRUMHEAD** AND THE RIM FROM YOUR DRUM. WIPE THE EDGE OF THE SHELL WITH A DRY CLOTH TO GET OFF ANY DIRT OR DUST. NEXT, PUT THE NEW HEAD ON THE DRUM AND THEN THE RIM OVER THAT.

2. **TIGHTEN THE LUGS BY HAND** UNTIL THEY'RE AS TIGHT AS YOU CAN GET THEM. WORK THE LUGS BY "GOING ACROSS THE DRUM AS YOU GO AROUND." START WITH THE LUG AT THE TOP (12 O'CLOCK POSITION), THEN GO TO THE LUG AT THE SIX O'CLOCK POSITION. GO TO THE THREE O'CLOCK POSITION, THEN TO THE NINE O'CLOCK POSITION, AND SO FORTH UNTIL YOU GO ALL THE WAY AROUND. THIS METHOD ENSURES THAT YOU TUNE THE HEAD EVENLY ON ALL SIDES.

3. **PRESS DOWN ON THE RIM OVER EACH LUG** AS YOU TIGHTEN IT FURTHER BY HAND, FOLLOWING THE SAME PATTERN AROUND THE DRUM.

4. AFTER ALL THE LUGS ARE FULLY TIGHTENED BY HAND, GENTLY **PRESS ON THE CENTER** OF THE HEAD WITH YOUR PALM UNTIL YOU HEAR SOME CRACKING FROM GLUE ON THE HEAD (BE CAREFUL NOT TO PUSH TOO HARD). THIS PUSHING SEATS THE HEAD AND FORCES IT TO MAKE FULL CONTACT WITH THE SHELL.

ROCK IT!

5. **USING THE DRUM KEY,** WORK AROUND THE DRUM IN THE SAME MANNER DESCRIBED IN PREVIOUS STEPS AND TIGHTEN EACH LUG ONE-QUARTER TO ONE-HALF A TURN UNTIL ALL THE WRINKLES ARE OUT OF THE HEAD. THIS PROCESS SHOULD TAKE ONLY ONE OR TWO TIMES AROUND THE DRUM.

6. **CHECK THE DRUM'S PITCH** (HOW HIGH OR LOW THE SOUND IS) BY HITTING THE DRUM IN THE CENTER OF THE HEAD.

7. **CONTINUE GOING AROUND** THE HEAD USING ONE-QUARTER TURNS UNTIL YOU GET TO A PITCH THAT RINGS FREELY.

RECORDING

THE OVERALL PROCESS OF RECORDING A BAND IN THE STUDIO BEGINS WITH LAYING DOWN SOLID DRUM TRACKS. ONCE THE DRUM TRACKS ARE RECORDED, THEN ALL THE OTHER TRACKS (GUITAR, BASS, VOCALS, ...) ARE BUILT UPON THE FOUNDATION THE DRUMS PROVIDE.

THE FIRST THING THAT WILL HAPPEN WHEN YOU GET INTO THE STUDIO IS MICING UP YOUR DRUM SET. BE PATIENT. IT TAKES TIME TO SET UP 6 TO 10 MICROPHONES. THE NEXT THING IS YOU WILL GET LEVELS AND DRUMS SOUNDS. BE PATIENT. THIS TAKES TIME TOO. REMEMEBER, THE DRUM TRACKS ARE THE FOUNDATION OF THE WHOLE REST OF THE RECORDING. GETTING GOOD SOUNDING DRUMS IS CRITICAL.

USUALLY YOUR DRUMS WILL BE SET UP IN ONE ROOM AND ALL THE GUITAR AMPLIFIERS WILL BE SET UP IN ANOTHER, SOUND-PROOFED ROOM. THAT WAY THE MICS ON THE DRUMS WON'T PICK UP THE SOUND FROM THE AMPLIFIERS. YOUR BANDMATES WILL BE IN THE ROOM WITH YOU, PLAYING THEIR INSTRUMENTS, BUT THEIR AMPS WILL BE IN THE OTHER ROOM. YOU WILL ALL BE ABLE TO HEAR THE AMPS AND EACH OTHER THROUGH THE HEADPHONES EVERYONE WEARS.

SOMETIMES IT REQUIRES A LOT OF "TAKES" TO GET A GOOD PERFORMANCE. BE COOL. IT CAN BE A LITTLE INTIMIDATING WITH ALL THE PRESSURE OF NEEDING TO GET PERFECT DRUM TRACKS. DON'T LET IT GET TO YOU. HAVE FUN! ENJOY MAKING MUSIC WITH YOUR BAND.

THEN YOU LEAVE AND THE ENGINEER "TIME CORRECTS" ALL THE DRUMS TO A PERFECT GRID IN PROTOOLS. MODERN RECORDING TECHNOLOGY ALLOWS THE ENGINEER TO TIGHTEN UP THE DRUMS SO THEY ARE ALMOST PERFECTLY IN TIME. THIS REQUIRES A LOT OF WORK AND SHOULD NOT ENCOURAGE SLOPPY OR INCONSISTENT DRUMMING.

AFTER THE DRUM TRACKS ARE DONE THEN YOU ARE DONE. NOW IT IS TIME FOR EVERYONE ELSE TO GO TO WORK — BUILDING THE SONG BASED ON YOUR DRUMS TRACKS. NOW IT BECOMES THE GUITAR AND BASS PLAYER AND SINGER'S TURN TO BE UNDER A MICROSCOPE!

IN THE STUDIO

CHALLENGES OF PLAYING IN THE STUDIO...

WHEN YOU GO INTO THE STUDIO TO RECORD YOU HAVE TO "FEEL" IT EVEN MORE BECAUSE IT IS GOING TO BE CAPTURED. IT SOUNDS BEST WHEN IT FEELS THE BEST. TO FEEL IT YOU NEED TO BE ABLE TO PLAY WITHOUT OVER THINKING WHAT YOU ARE DOING. THAT IS WHY YOU NEED TO PRACTICE AND KNOW YOUR PARTS BEFORE YOU GO INTO THE STUDIO.

THE CLICK TRACK...

YOUR ASSIGNMENT (SHOULD YOU ACCEPT IT) IS TO FIND THE GROOVE WITHIN THE STEADY BEAT OF THE CLICK TRACK. (SEE "PLAYING IN THE POCKET.") TO BE ABLE TO DO THIS YOU MUST PRACTICE WITH A METRONOME/CLICK BEFORE GOING INTO THE STUDIO.
THERE ARE MANY FREE METRONOME APPS FOR YOUR PHONE.

DO'S AND DON'TS IN THE STUDIO.....

DO YOUR HOMEWORK... LISTEN TO THE MATERIAL BEFORE THE SESSION. PRACTICE IT AS MUCH AS YOU CAN. FIGURE OUT WHERE YOU ARE GOING TO PUT YOUR FILLS BEFOREHAND.

CHANGE THE DRUM HEADS AND TUNE YOUR DRUMS **BEFORE** YOU GO IN THE STUDIO. PUT NEW SKINS ON ALL THE BATTER SIDES.

WHEN THE DRUM SET GETS MIC'D UP YOU HEAR THINGS YOU DIDN'T HEAR BEFORE: LITTLE RATTLES, PEDALS SQUEAKING, OUT-OF-TUNE HEADS...

MAKE SURE NOTHING IS LOOSE AND RATTLING **BEFORE** YOU GO INTO THE STUDIO. TIGHTEN ALL THE SCREWS, BOLTS, AND WINGNUTS.

LUBRICATE THE HINGES AND MOVING PARTS ON THE KICK PEDAL AND HI-HAT PEDAL SO THEY DO NOT SQUEAK.

BRING EXTRAS OF EVERYTHING: HEADS (ESPECIALLY A SPARE SNARE HEAD), STICKS, FELTS, WASHERS, BASS DRUM BEATER...

THE NIGHT BEFORE EAT A HEARTY/HEALTHY DINNER, GET A GOOD NIGHTS REST, AND EAT A HEARTY/HEALTHY BREAKFAST.

MICING THE DRUM SET

BASS DRUM – USE A LARGE DIAPHRAGM DYNAMIC MICROPHONE. PUT A PILLOW OR BLANKET INSIDE THE DRUM TO REDUCE BOOMINESS. YOU CAN PLACE THE MIC INSIDE THE DRUM NEAR THE INSIDE HEAD FOR A SHARP ATTACK, HALFWAY INSIDE THE DRUM GIVES YOU MORE BODY, OR NEAR THE OUTSIDE HEAD TO BE MORE BOOMY.

SNARE DRUM – USE A SHURE SM57 CARDIOD MICROPHONE. TO GET A GOOD, PUNCHY SNARE DRUM SOUND, PLACE THE MIC 1 TO 2 INCHES AWAY FROM THE DRUM HEAD WITH THE MIC POINTED DIRECTLY AT THE HEAD. ADDING COMPRESSION TO THE SNARE DRUM IS CRITICAL.

HI-HATS – USE A SMALL DIAPHRAGM CONDENSER MICROPHONE. PLACE THE MIC ABOUT 3 TO 4 INCHES ABOVE THE TOP HI-HAT CYMBAL. POINT IT DOWN TOWARD THE CYMBAL. THE EXACT PLACEMENT OF THE MIC IS LESS IMPORTANT THAN THE PLACEMENT OF THE OTHER INSTRUMENT MICS BECAUSE OF THE HI-HATS' TONE. JUST MAKE SURE YOUR MIC ISN'T SO CLOSE THAT YOU HIT IT.

TOMS – USE A DYNAMIC MICROPHONE. FOR THE MOUNTED TOMS (THE ONES ABOVE THE KICK DRUM), YOU CAN USE ONE OR TWO MICS. IF YOU USE ONE MIC, PLACE IT BETWEEN THE TWO DRUMS ABOUT 4 TO 6 INCHES AWAY FROM THE HEADS . IF YOU USE TWO MICS, PLACE ONE ABOVE EACH DRUM ABOUT 1 TO 3 INCHES ABOVE THE HEAD.

CYMBALS – USE A SMALL DIAPHRAGM CONDENSER MICROPHONE. PLACE THE MICS ABOUT 6 INCHES ABOVE EACH CYMBAL. PLAYING THE CYMBALS SOFTLY ALLOWS YOU TO GET MORE OF THE DRUMS IN THESE MICS. THIS HELPS THE DRUMS SOUND BIGGER.

OVERHEADS – USE A PAIR OF DIAPHRAGM CONDENSER MICROPHONES TO PICK UP THE HIGH FREQUENCIES OF THE CYMBALS AND THE "AIR" FROM THE DRUMS. THE OVERHEADS CAPTURE THE AMBIENCE AND THE SPACE OF THE DRUMS. PLACE THE MICS 1 TO 2 FEET ABOVE THE CYMBALS AND 3 TO 6 FEET APART. POINT THE MIC DOWN TOWARDS THE DRUMS.

THE ROOM – IF YOU WANT A BIG DRUM SOUND YOU NEED A BIG ROOM. THE ROOM INFLUENCES THE SOUND OF THE DRUMS MORE THAN ANY OTHER INSTRUMENT. THE ROOM DOES NOT NEED TO BE A "ROOM" – JOHN BONHAM SET HIS DRUMS UP AT THE BOTTOM OF A HUGE STAIRCASE IN A CASTLE IN ENGLAND TO GET THE FAMOUS DRUM SOUND HEARD ON "WHEN THE LEVEE BREAKS" FROM "LED ZEPPELIN IV."

CYMBALS
SMALL DIAPHRAGM CONDENSER MIC

CYMBALS
SMALL DIAPHRAGM CONDENSER MIC

TOMS
DYNAMIC MIC

FLOOR TOMS
DYNAMIC MIC

BASS
LARGE DIAPHRAGM DYNAMIC MIC

HI-HAT CYMBALS
SMALL DIAPHRAGM CONDENSER MIC

SNARE
SHURE SM57 CARDIOD MIC

ON STAGE

SOUND CHECK

SOUND CHECK IS NOT DRUM SOLO TIME!

IF YOUR BAND GETS THE CHANCE TO SOUND CHECK BEFORE THE GIG, LISTEN TO THE SOUNDMAN AND PLAY ONLY WHAT HE TELLS YOU TO PLAY .... USUALLY HE WILL ASK YOU TO PLAY THE KICK DRUM, THEN THE SNARE DRUM, THEN THE TOMS, AND THEN THE CYMBALS.

HIT THE DRUMS NICE AND SLOW (QUARTER NOTES) SO THE SOUNDMAN CAN HEAR THE WHOLE TONE. HIT THE DRUMS WITH THE SAME FORCE THAT YOU WILL USE WHEN YOU ARE PERFORMING, OTHERWISE THE SOUNDMAN WILL NOT GET AN ACCURATE LEVEL. TRY TO BE AS EFFICIENT AS POSSIBLE, REMEMBER EVERYONE ELSE NEEDS TO SOUNDCHECK ALSO.

THE CHALLENGE OF PLAYING LIVE ON STAGE...

DON'T GET TOO AMPED UP AND PUSH ALL THE TEMPOS. WHEN THERE ARE 50, OR 500, (OR 50,000!) SCREAMING FANS ALL DIRECTING THEIR ENERGY AT THE STAGE, YOUR HEART STARTS BEATING FAST AND IT'S VERY EASY TO GET EXCITED AND PLAY TOO FAST. REMEMBER ... YOU ARE THE TIMEKEEPER. THE BAND IS DEPENDING ON YOU TO KEEP THE TEMPO THAT YOU PRACTICED 100 TIMES.

USE DYNAMICS – DIFFERENCES IN VOLUME AND TEMPO MAKE THE MUSIC INTERESTING TO THE LISTENER. PLAY SOFTER DURING THE VERSES AND COME UP DURING THE CHORUS.

MAKE AN EFFORT TO PULL THE GROOVE BACK IN CERTAIN SECTIONS OF THE SHOW (USUALLY DURING A BALLAD OR BUSY FILL). COUNT THE SUBDIVISIONS IN THE BEAT; THE 1/8TH OR 1/16TH NOTES INSTEAD OF JUST THE 1/4 NOTES. THE MORE YOU DO IT, THE EASIER IT BECOMES.

PERFORMANCE TIPS

PRACTICING YOUR RUDIMENTS, FILLS, LICKS, AND BEATS ALONE CAN GET BORING. JUST REMEMBER, YOU ARE PRACTICING FOR THE TIME WHEN YOU CAN GET TOGETHER WITH YOUR FRIENDS AND JAM. PLAYING MUSIC WITH YOUR FRIENDS IS SO MUCH FUN! EVEN MORE FUN IS PLAYING MUSIC WITH YOUR FRIENDS IN FRONT OF AN AUDIENCE!

IF YOU STEP ON THE STAGE YOU HAVE A RESPONSIBILITY TO THE AUDIENCE TO BE PREPARED AND DO YOUR BEST TO GIVE THEM A GREAT SHOW. THAT MEANS YOU USE ALL OF YOUR TALENT AND IMAGINATION TO ENGAGE AND ENTERTAIN YOUR AUDIENCE.

PRACTICE THE WAY YOU WANT TO PLAY. PRACTICE IN YOUR GARAGE THE SAME WAY YOU WANT TO PLAY ON STAGE. IF YOU PRACTICE WITH YOUR HEAD HANGING DOWN AND EYES CLOSED, THEN THAT IS THE WAY YOU WILL PLAY WHEN YOU ARE ON THE STAGE. PRETEND EVERY PRACTICE IS A DRESS REHEARSAL.

LOOK AT THE AUDIENCE. EYE CONTACT WITH YOUR AUDIENCE IS VERY IMPORTANT.

LET THE AUDIENCE LOOK AT YOU. SET UP YOUR CYMBALS SO PEOPLE CAN SEE YOU.

AND WOULD IT KILL YOU TO SMILE A LITTLE BIT? GIVE A SMILE AND A NOD TO THE PEOPLE YOU KNOW IN THE AUDIENCE.

PLAYING ON STAGE CAN BE INTIMIDATING AT FIRST, BUT LIKE EVERYTHING ELSE WITH THE DRUMS, IT BECOMES EASIER AFTER YOU'VE DONE IT A FEW TIMES. PLAY ON STAGE AS OFTEN AS YOU CAN AND YOU WILL GET BETTER AND BETTER AT IT.

JOHN BONHAM, BILL WARD, NEIL PEART, LARS ULRICH AND ALL THE OTHER ROCK STARS LOOK TOTALLY AT HOME ON STAGE. THEY DIDN'T START OUT THAT WAY. TO BE COMFORTABLE ON STAGE YOU NEED THE CONFIDENCE THAT ONLY COMES FROM EXPERIENCE.

SEE AS MANY LIVE CONCERTS AS YOU CAN. WATCH VIDEOS OF YOUR FAVORITE BANDS TO SEE HOW THEY DO IT.

PRACTICE THE WAY YOU WANT TO PLAY!

DON'T ACT LIKE A ZOMBIE ON STAGE!

DAVE GROHL

DAVID ERIC GROHL WAS BORN ON JANUARY 14, 1969 IN WARREN, OHIO.

DAVE BEGAN LEARNING TO PLAY GUITAR WHEN HE WAS 12 YEARS OLD. HE QUICKLY GREW TIRED OF LESSONS AND TAUGHT HIMSELF INSTEAD.

DAVE'S COUSIN INTRODUCED HIM TO PUNK ROCK BY TAKING HIM TO PUNK ROCK SHOWS. HIS FIRST CONCERT WAS IN 1982 TO SEE "NAKED RAYGUN" AT "THE CUBBY BEAR" IN CHICAGO WHEN HE WAS 13 YEARS OLD.

WHILE IN HIGH SCHOOL, DAVE PLAYED GUITAR IN SEVERAL LOCAL BANDS. HE TAUGHT HIMSELF TO PLAY DRUMS BY PLAYING "AIR DRUMS" ON PILLOWS ALONG TO JOHN BONHAM.

DAVE DECIDED TO SWITCH TO PLAYING DRUMS, AND PLAYED IN SEVERAL BANDS WITH FRIENDS.

WHEN DAVE WAS 17, HE AUDITIONED FOR THE WASHINGTON D.C. BAND "SCREAM." TO DAVE'S SURPRISE, THE BAND ASKED HIM TO JOIN. DAVE LEFT SCHOOL AND OVER THE NEXT FOUR YEARS, DAVE TOURED EXTENSIVELY WITH SCREAM, RECORDING TWO STUDIO ALBUMS AND A COUPLE OF LIVE ALBUMS.

DAVE BECAME A FAN OF THE SEATTLE BAND "MELVINS" AND BECAME FRIENDS WITH THE MELVINS' SINGER/GUITAR PLAYER, BUZZ OSBORNE. WHEN SCREAM PLAYED A GIG IN SEATTLE IN 1990, BUZZ TOOK HIS FRIENDS, KURT COBAIN AND KRIST NOVOSELIC, TO SEE SCREAM PLAY.

WHEN SCREAM BROKE UP IN LATE 1990, DAVE CALLED BUZZ FOR ADVICE. AT THE TIME "NIRVANA" WAS LOOKING FOR A NEW DRUMMER. BUZZ GAVE DAVE'S PHONE NUMBER TO KRIST NOVOSELIC, WHO INVITED DAVE TO SEATTLE TO AUDITION FOR NIRVANA. DAVE SOON JOINED THEM FULL-TIME.

WHEN DAVE JOINED NIRVANA, THE BAND HAD ALREADY RECORDED DEMOS FOR THEIR NEXT RECORD. DAVE SPENT THE FIRST COUPLE MONTHS WITH NIRVANA TRAVELING TO DIFFERENT RECORD COMPANIES AS THE BAND SHOPPED FOR A MAJOR LABEL RECORD DEAL. NIRVANA EVENTUALLY SIGNED WITH DGC RECORDS AND ENTERED THE STUDIO IN 1991 TO RECORD THEIR SECOND ALBUM.

DAVE WAS 22 WHEN "NEVERMIND" WAS RELEASED IN 1991. THE ALBUM BECAME A HUGE SUCCESS AND CATAPULTED NIRVANA AND ITS MEMBERS TO WORLDWIDE STARDOM.

BUYING DRUMS

BUY THE BEST EQUIPMENT YOU CAN AFFORD – IT WILL BE EASIER TO PLAY, IT WILL SOUND BETTER, AND IF TAKEN CARE OF PROPERLY IT WILL LAST FOR YEARS AND RETAIN ITS VALUE. USED EQUIPMENT IS A GREAT WAY TO GET GOOD GEAR CHEAP.

FIND OUT WHAT YOUR FAVORITE DRUMMER PLAYS.... THE BRAND, WHAT SIZE THE DRUMS ARE, THE TYPES OF CYMBALS THEY USE ... EVEN A BUDGET VERSION OF THEIR SET-UP WILL GET YOU CLOSE TO THE SOUND YOU WANT.

SHOP AROUND. PLAY ALL THE DIFFERENT SETS YOU LIKE. DON'T GO BY THE LOOKS – GO BY THE SOUND. USE YOUR EARS, NOT YOUR EYES.

DRUMS: TYPE OF WOOD... DRUM SHELLS ARE MADE BY GLUING BETWEEN 6 AND 9 THIN LAYERS OF WOOD TOGETHER. THE MOST COMMON TYPES OF WOOD USED TO MAKE DRUMS ARE MAPLE AND BIRCH. MAPLE HAS A LOUD, BRIGHT TONE. MAPLE IS "LIVELY" AND "OPEN." BIRCH HAS A MELLOWER TONE. BIRCH IS "TIGHT," "THICK," AND "PUNCHY." SOME DRUMMERS USE A MIX OF MAPLE AND BIRCH: A MAPLE KICK AND SNARE WITH BIRCH TOMS.

CYMBALS... THICKNESS IS THE BIGGEST THING TO LOOK FOR IN CYMBALS. THINNER CYMBALS ARE BRIGHT AND, WELL, "THIN." THICKER CYMBALS ARE HEAVY, LOUD, AND DURABLE. (PERFECT FOR ROCK AND METAL!) THE HI-HATS ARE THE MOST IMPORTANT CYMBALS BECAUSE YOU PLAY THEM ALL THE TIME. BUY A THICKER PAIR OF 13-14 INCH HI-HATS. THICK CRASH CYMBALS ARE LOUD AND HAVE A LOT OF SUSTAIN. A THICK RIDE CYMBAL WILL GIVE YOU A NICE BELL SOUND ("TING").

FOOT PEDALS... THE KICK DRUM PEDAL/S, THE HI-HAT STAND... THESE ARE WHAT YOU "WORK" AND WHAT YOU "FEEL." INVEST IN GOOD PEDALS. THEY WILL LAST LONGER AND MAKE PLAYING EASIER AND MORE FUN.

HARDWARE... GET THE HEAVIEST STANDS YOU CAN AFFORD. LOOK FOR "DOUBLE-BRACED" LEGS FOR YOUR STANDS. PAYING A LITTLE MORE FOR GOOD STANDS IS WORTH IT. THEN YOUR CRASH CYMBAL WON'T FALL OVER EVERY TIME YOU GIVE IT A GOOD HIT, AND YOU WON'T NEED TO ADJUST THE SNARE STAND ALL THE TIME.

WHAT TO LOOK OUT FOR WHEN BUYING **USED GEAR...** MAKE SURE THE CYMBALS ARE NOT CRACKED AND THE DRUMS ARE NOT WARPED. LOOK TO SEE IF THERE IS ANY RUST OR A LOT OF DUST. THIS MEANS THEY PROBABLY WERE NOT STORED OR TAKEN CARE OF PROPERLY.

THE GREAT DRUMMERS...
- ~ PRACTICED ALL THE TIME WHEN THEY WERE YOUNG.
- ~ WERE PASSIONATE ABOUT PLAYING THE DRUMS.
- ~ PLAYED IN BANDS WHEN THEY WERE TEENAGERS.
- ~ WROTE ORIGINAL SONGS.
- ~ NEVER GOT DISCOURAGED.
- ~ RECORDED THEIR FIRST RECORDS WHEN THEY WERE IN THEIR EARLY 20'S.

LEARN AS MUCH AS YOU CAN FROM THE GREAT PLAYERS, BUT ALSO WORK TO DEVELOP YOUR OWN STYLE AND IDENTITY AS A DRUMMER.

LEARNING TO PLAY THE DRUMS REQUIRES **A LOT OF PRACTICE.** REPETITION CREATES...
MUSCLE MEMORY ...
AFTER A WHILE YOUR MUSCLES WILL REMEMBER WHAT TO DO AND YOU WON'T HAVE TO THINK ABOUT IT.

ROCK OUT!

TO IMPROVE YOUR TECHNIQUE ... **PRACTICE.**
TO IMPROVE YOUR EAR .... LISTEN.
TO IMPROVE YOUR MIND .... **STUDY.**
TO IMPROVE YOUR SOUL .... **LEARN.**

TO IMPROVE YOUR **MUSIC** ....
IMPROVE YOUR **TECHNIQUE, EAR, MIND,** AND **SOUL.**

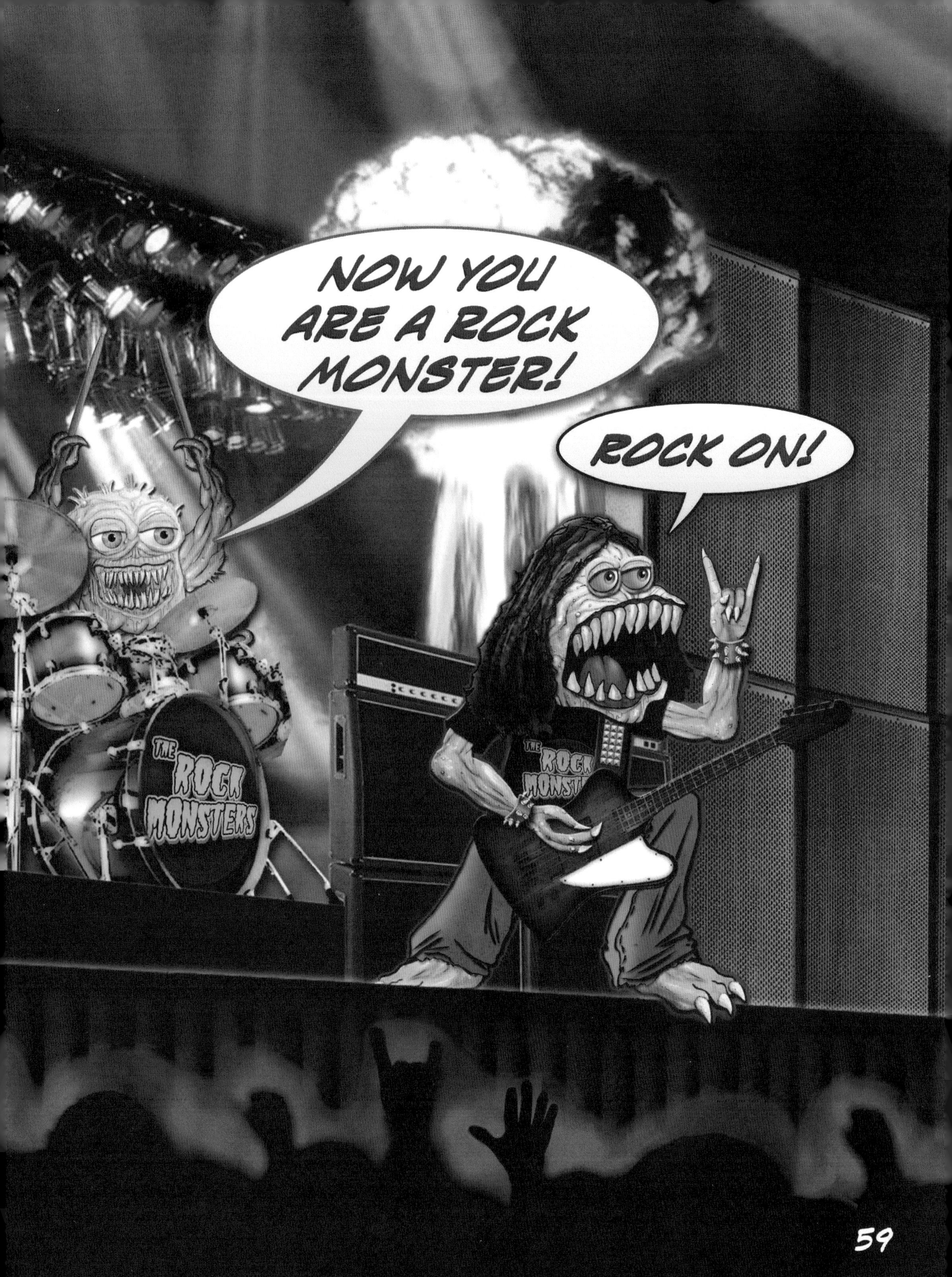
NOW YOU ARE A ROCK MONSTER!
ROCK ON!
THE ROCK MONSTERS

GUIDE FOR PARENTS

THE SUCCESS OF YOUR FUTURE ROCK STAR LEARNING TO PLAY THE DRUMS DEPENDS ON YOUR ENCOURAGEMENT AND HELP. HERE ARE SOME TIPS TO HELP YOU HELP THEM ...

1. START WITH A "5 -PIECE KIT" - FIND OUT WHAT YOUR ROCK MONSTER'S FAVORITE DRUMMER PLAYS... THE BRAND, THE SIZE THE DRUMS ARE, THE TYPES OF CYMBALS THEY USE ... EVEN A BUDGET VERSION OF THEIR SET-UP WILL GET YOUR ROCK MONSTER CLOSE TO THE SOUND THEY WANT.

2. FOOT PEDALS... THE KICK DRUM PEDAL/S, THE HI-HAT STAND... THESE ARE WHAT THE DRUMMER "WORKS" AND WHAT THEY "FEEL." USUALLY AN INEXPENSIVE DRUM SET WILL COME WITH A CHEAP BASS DRUM PEDAL AND A CHEAP HI-HAT STAND. INVEST IN GOOD PEDALS. THEY WILL LAST LONGER AND MAKE PLAYING EASIER AND MORE FUN.

3. BUY THE BEST EQUIPMENT YOU CAN AFFORD - IT WILL BE EASIER TO PLAY, IT WILL SOUND BETTER, AND IF TAKEN CARE OF PROPERLY IT WILL LAST FOR YEARS AND RETAIN ITS VALUE. USED EQUIPMENT IS A GREAT WAY TO GET GOOD GEAR CHEAP. THINGS WERE BUILT BETTER 10 YEARS AGO.

4. FIND A GOOD DRUM TEACHER - THIS IS CRITICAL TO THEIR DEVELOPMENT AS A MUSICIAN. MAKE SURE THE TEACHER WILL TEACH THEM WHAT THEY WANT TO LEARN. IF YOUR KID WANTS TO LEARN METALLICA, A TEACHER WHO IS NOT INTO METAL IS NOT GOING TO BE THE BEST FIT. IF YOUR KID IS HAPPY WITH THE TEACHER AND WHAT THE TEACHER IS TEACHING, THEY'LL BE MUCH MORE LIKELY TO HAVE FUN AND LEARN.

5. OFFER AN INCENTIVE - OFFER TO BUY THEM A NEW CYMBAL, OR BASS DRUM PEDAL, OR STICK BAG ~ WHATEVER WILL MOTIVATE THEM, IF THEY LEARN TO PLAY A DIFFICULT SONG ALL THE WAY THROUGH PERFECTLY. (MAKE SURE THE GOAL IS ATTAINABLE BUT REQUIRES SOME WORK.)

6. LET YOUR ROCK MONSTER HAVE 30 MINUTES A DAY TO WAIL ON THEIR DRUMS. YOUR ROCK MONSTER NEEDS TO DEVELOP THEIR STRENGTH AND STAMINA TO PREPARE FOR THE TIME WHEN THEY CAN GET TOGETHER WITH A BAND AND MAKE SOME REAL NOISE! (P.S. BUY SOME EAR PLUGS!)ENJOY!

Rock History 101

1930	**DELTA BLUES**	CHARLEY PATTON, SON HOUSE, LEADBELLY, BUKKAH WHITE
1935	**ROBERT JOHNSON**	NATIONAL RESONATOR GUITARS
		STELLA ACOUSTIC GUITARS
		RADIO AND 78 RPM PHONOGRAPH RECORDS
1940	**WORLD WAR II**	**THE GREAT MIGRATION FROM SOUTH TO NORTH**
1945		RAY CHARLES, FATS DOMINO, LOUIS JORDAN, T-BONE WALKER
	RHYTHM & BLUES	CHICAGO BLUES – **MUDDY WATERS**, HOWLIN' WOLF, ---
1950		THE 3 KINGS: B.B. KING, ALBERT KING, FREDDIE KING.
		FENDER TELECASTER GUITAR INVENTED. FENDER AMPS.
1955	**ROCK N' ROLL**	**ELVIS PRESLEY** **CHUCK BERRY**
1957		
		LITTLE RICHARD, JERRY LEE LEWIS, BUDDY HOLLY, BILL HALEY, BO DIDDLEY,
1958		SUN RECORDS, FENDER STRATOCASTER GUITAR, AM RADIO & 45 RPM RECORDS
1962	**BOB DYLAN**	SONGWRITERS BECOME POETIC, PERSONAL, AND POLITICAL.
1963	**THE BEATLES**	**BRITISH INVASION** **THE ROLLING STONES**
1965		THE YARDBIRDS, THE KINKS, THE WHO, THE ANIMALS ---
1967	**JIMI HENDRIX**	THE BYRDS, THE GRATEFUL DEAD, THE DOORS
		CREAM ~ ERIC CLAPTON **GIBSON** GTRS. **Marshall AMPLIFIERS**
1969	**LED ZEPPELIN**	
1970	**CLASSIC ROCK**	AEROSMITH, AC/DC, BLACK SABBATH, PINK FLOYD, BAD CO.
		DEEP PURPLE, THE FACES, HUMBLE PIE, THIN LIZZY, RUSH
		LYNYRD SKYNYRD, MONTROSE, KISS, CHEAP TRICK, ZZ TOP
1975		FM RADIO, 8-TRACK TAPES, AND LP RECORDS POPULAR
1977	**PUNK ROCK**	THE CLASH, SEX PISTOLS, THE RAMONES **BOB MARLEY**
1978	**VAN HALEN**	**NEW WAVE OF BRITISH HEAVY METAL**
1980	**RANDY RHOADS**	JUDAS PRIEST, UFO, MOTÖRHEAD, IRON MAIDEN, DEF LEPPARD
1985	**THRASH METAL** **METALLICA**	MEGADETH, SLAYER, ANTHRAX **STEVIE RAY VAUGHAN**
1987	**SUNSET STRIP**	MÖTLEY CRÜE, RATT, POISON--- **GUNS N' ROSES** **MTV C D'S**
1990	**GRUNGE** **NIRVANA**	PEARL JAM, SOUNDGARDEN, ALICE IN CHAINS---
1995	**MODERN ROCK NU-METAL**	FOO FIGHTERS, RED HOT CHILI PEPPERS, GREEN DAY, ---
2000		PANTERA, KORN, TOOL, RAGE AGAINST THE MACHINE --- MP3'S
2010		THE WHITE STRIPES, QUEENS OF THE STONE AGE, LAMB OF GOD, MASTODON, AVENGED SEVENFOLD --- IPOD'S
2015		**!!!!!! YOU ARE THE NEXT CHAPTER IN ROCK HISTORY !!!!!!**

Printed in Great Britain
by Amazon